The Waning of Humaneness

KONRAD LORENZ

The Waning of Humaneness

TRANSLATED FROM THE GERMAN
BY ROBERT WARREN KICKERT

LITTLE, BROWN AND COMPANY
BOSTON   TORONTO

Library of Congress Cataloging-in-Publication Data
Lorenz, Konrad, 1903–
The waning of humaneness.

Translation of: Der Abbau des Menschlichen.
1. Man.   2. Civilization, Modern — 1950–
I. Title.
BD450.L586413   1987   128   86-27470

NOTE: During the translation of this book, the original
German text was revised and augmented by the author,
translator, and copyeditor.

RRD VA

Designed by Robert G. Lowe

*Published simultaneously in Canada
by Little, Brown & Company (Canada) Limited*

PRINTED IN THE UNITED STATES OF AMERICA

Contents

The Waning of Humaneness

A Very Brief Foreword

Now, as never before, the prospects for a human future are exceptionally dismal. Most probably the human race will soon and swiftly, but certainly not painlessly, be committed to suicide through use of extant nuclear weaponry. Even if this does not happen, every human being remains in peril of a slow death through poisoning and desiccating the environment in which he lives and by which he is sustained. Even if, just in time, humans should somehow impose a check on their blind and unbelievably stupid conduct, they still remain threatened by a progressive decline of all those attributes and attainments that constitute their humanity. Many concerned people have pointed out these dangers and many of their books contain the recognition that destruction of the environment and cultural "decadence" go hand in hand. Yet only a few of them regard the waning of humaneness as a malady; only a few, as Aldous Huxley has done, continue onward in search of the causes and possible remedial measures. The book presented here is intended to serve this search.

A Very Short Summary

Part One: Many people believe that the course taken by everything that happens in the world is predetermined and directed toward some purpose. Actually, the processes of organic creation are realized in unforeseeable ways. On this realization, this recognition, is based our belief both in the possibility of truly creative processes and in the freedom of human choice, but above all in the *responsibility* of every human being. For this reason the first part of this book takes on the task of refuting the assumption that what happens in the world is predetermined. If what happens were predetermined, there would be, basically, no history of creation, no genesis at all.

Part Two: Since all of the moral responsibilities of humans are determined by their perceptions of values, the epidemic delusion that only numerical and measurable reality has validity must be confronted and contradicted. What must be made clear, and convincingly, is that our subjective experiential processes possess the same degree of reality as everything that can be expressed in the terminologies of the exact natural sciences.

Part Three: Capacities for conceptual thought and verbal language, in other words, the workings of the human mind, have brought about an accumulation of knowledge, of capabilities, and of aspirations whose exponentially increasing volume is so enormous that the mind can truly be regarded as the "adversary of the soul." The human mind is capable of contriving conditions with which the natural constitution of humans can no longer cope. Given this circumstance, some culturally acquired as well as some "instinctive," genetically programmed norms of behavior, although still virtues and effective qualities during the recent historical past, have become, instead, detriments leading to destruction.

Part Four: Here concern focuses on the predicament into which the processes described in Part Three have led us. The situation is menacing. Room for hope does remain despite the irreversible vicious-circularity of some aspects of technical and economic development. Thought habits engendered by technology have become consolidated into doctrines of the technocratic system, which has isolated and protected itself through self-immunization. Technocracy, as a result, has become overorganizational and its enervating effect increases with the number of people to be organized. An absence of those multifarious interchanges that are prerequisites for every creative development is also obvious within the cultural realm.

The predicament of young people today is especially critical. Forestalling the threatening apocalypse will devolve on their perceptions of value; their sensibilities of the beautiful and worthwhile must be aroused and renewed. And just these values are those being suppressed by scientism and technomorphic thinking.

Educative measures begin with an exercising of *Gestalt* (form) perception, our only means for achieving a sensitivity to harmonies. In order for this perception to function properly, it must, as must any computing mechanism, be provided with an immense amount of data. The closest possible contact with the living natural world at the earliest possible age is the most promising way to achieve this proper function.

PART ONE

Freedom
in Evolution

···⊰[ONE]⊱···

The Belief
in a Purpose-Oriented World

ITS DEMORALIZING CONSEQUENCES

Pierre Teilhard de Chardin took the most significant step when he equated creation with evolution. His recognition that every evolutionary development was coupled to a *value increment* is just as fundamental for our view of the world as it was for his. He also believed, however, that the tack taken by evolution from the inorganic to the organic, and from the lower forms to the higher forms, was principally predestined, *predetermined* — just as Oswald Spengler believed in an unavoidable decline as the destiny of our culture.

These two contrasting views have the same effect for human behavior: both permit humans to feel released from any responsibility for what happens in the world. The determining factors of organic development, primarily genetic change (mutation) and choice (selection), have produced the human mind as well as all other living phenomena. But the human mind has since found ways and means of switching off the most important of the determinant factors that caused its own creation — remorseless, preserving selection. Evolution lifted humans up onto their feet, placed them in an unstable situation (in a profoundly symbolical sense), and then took its hands away. Creative selection, a subject to which Part Four of this book is dedicated, has ceased to influence humans. Creative selection has been replaced by intraspecific selection, and we already know precisely some of the bizarre garden paths down which intraspecific selection can lead species change.

In a certain sense, in the phylogenetic sense, it is permissible to say that creative evolution has ceased on our earth. Human cultural development goes on at an ever-increasing rate and has now reached such a velocity that it is hardly an exaggeration to maintain that the tempo of genetic, phylogenetic evolution, by comparison, can be regarded as negligible, can, in fact, be equated with nil. In any case, the alterations brought about upon the entire planet through human cultural development are carried out at a rate that completely rules out phylogenetic development keeping pace with it, or even being "towed along" behind. Because of this disjunction, humans are, in the highest degree, an endangered species.

"Die ewig rege, die heilsam schaffende Gewalt" [The perpetually stirring, the curative creative force], as Goethe called it, can be effective today exclusively through man's sense of values. The decision whether the evolution of organic life here and now is to go "downward" or "upward" has become the responsibility of mankind. Without a sense of values, questions concerning the consequences of our actions can lead neither to commandments nor to prohibitions.

No one knows if the further phylogenetic development of humans will continue to lead upward at all. I, however, steadfastly believe in this possibility. If cultural development, despite running along at a rate immensely faster than phylogenesis, continues to remain subject to laws similar to those followed by phylogenesis, then it is very probable that it is also capable of turning the direction of phylogenesis toward its own inclinations, that is, in the same direction. Yet this direction now appears, in the light of our present technocratic world order, to be leading indubitably downward. If this is so, then human existence is imperiled.

THE ERRONEOUS BELIEF IN SO-CALLED PROGRESS

Although many people are already fully aware of the dangers technological developments call down onto the heads of all mankind, there are also countless others, "technomorphic"-thinking humans, who are firmly convinced that every development generates, of necessity, new values. Even if one thinks in Goethe's terms, confining the conceptualization of development to his definition as differentiation and subordination of component parts, this view remains false and much more so with regard to possible cultural developments than with reference to phylogenesis.

Although the genesis of values has, in fact, development as a prerequisite, value formation is not necessarily the logical consequence of development. Within a technocratic world order, the actions taken during the accomplishment of development determine the very conception of values. In an unfortunately circumscribed sense, actions become the essence of value creation. The means become the end.

This can be especially well illustrated by taking, as an example, what is understood in the United States when talking about developing a piece of property. "To develop an area" means, on the piece of land in question, to radically destroy all of the natural vegetation and to cover the ground thus exposed with concrete or macadam or, less crass, with a park lawn. If a stretch of sea beach or lakefront is available, this is reinforced by constructing a cement wall. If a brook or stream is present, its natural winding course is straightened and regulated or, if possible, contained within a conduit. Then the entire area is "sanitized," that is, poisoned by spraying pesticides. Finally this piece of developed real estate is sold to some subdued, urbanized, and stupefied consumer at the highest possible price. Technomorphic thinking has confused, over and above this, and in an almost compulsively neurotic manner, the mere existence of the possibility of realizing a particular process technically with the obligation actually to carry the possibility through. It has just about become a "must" of the technocratic religion: everything that is at all possible to do should by all possible means be done.

Certainly I exaggerate. Nevertheless, even today, a vast majority of people continue to delude themselves with the belief that the advances of our civilization must, necessarily, and in a predestined way, lead to an enhancement of values.

THE REJECTION OF A WORLD NOT PURPOSE-ORIENTED

To many people it seems to be unthinkable that in the universe there might be processes that are not directed toward specific ends and goals. Because we regard our own meaningless actions as worthless, it disturbs us that there could be some events suspended above any ultimate significance. Goethe lets Faust say, while watching sea waves surging and breaking into foam: *"Was zur Verzweiflung mich beängstigen könnte, zwecklose Kraft unbändiger Elemente."* [What could disquiet me to despair, the purposeless power of intractable elements.] But most of all, man's feeling of self-confidence is injured by the consideration that cosmic events are absolutely indifferent to him and all his concerns. Because he can observe in the ways of the world around him that the meaningless predominates, he fears that, in itself and purely quantitatively, the meaningless could triumph over all human efforts to provide sense and significance. From this fear wells the compulsion to presume that everything happening must have a hidden meaning. As Nicolai Hartmann has said, "Man does not want to face the hardness of reality as something absolutely indifferent to him. He would conclude that life was not worth living." In another context this philosopher says: "Man has not even the slightest intention of ever nearing the suspicion that imparting meaning should be a priority of humans, and that perhaps through his own disinclination, it is he alone who might be the one who has disinherited himself from this priority."

Paradoxically, the recoil from a world of events not purpose-oriented, not ultimately deterministic, is also motivated by the fear that the free will of humans might prove to be an illusion, a fear that is not only epistemologically nonsensical but also (as far as a purpose-oriented world is concerned) completely turned around. "Accepting, as if it were without contradiction, the conceptualization of a world that, from its very inception, is completely and ultimately predetermined, coercively excludes every human freedom" and limits man to the behavior of a vehicle restricted to tracks, forced by set constraints to reach its goal — if it does not derail beforehand. Such a conceptualization would signify an absolute disavowal of humans as responsible beings.

THE THREE KINDS OF PURPOSE-ORIENTED ACTION

Processes determined by an ultimate end or goal exist in the cosmos exclusively within the realm of the organic. A categorical analysis of the ultimate nexus, in the sense implied by Nicolai Hartmann, can only be initiated by means of insight into the effective interactions of "links" in a very specific chain of events.

Three characteristic actions are involved that, indeed, cannot actually be separated from one another or examined independently since they form a functional, integrated unit: first, the setting of a goal, which incorporates "skipping" spaces of imagined time in anticipation of something happening in the future; second, a choice of means, which follows the goal setting and is, thus, to a certain extent, reflexively determined by the goal; and third, a realization of the set goal through the causal, sequential unfolding of the chosen means.

Nicolai Hartmann has emphasized strongly that there must always be on hand a "carrier" for the action, a "setter" for the goal, and a "chooser" for the means. In addition, the "third act," the realization of the goal, must usually be "watched over" since, through the choice of means, mistakes might have been made and, in this case, when a deviation from the predetermined line appears at any point in the series, corrections must be made through new means.

Nicolai Hartmann believes that the carrier of the action and the setter of the goal can only be, must always be, a "consciousness" because, as he says, ". . . only a consciousness has maneuverability within conceptual time, can leap beyond sequential time, can predetermine, anticipate, choose means and, retrospectively, go back in thought over the

skipped spaces through to the 'first one' at the beginning."
Since the time Nicolai Hartmann wrote those lines, research
into the biochemistry of morphogenesis and ethological research into the appetitive behavior of animals have revealed
processes that are certainly not associated with consciousness but which conform to the required three acts in their
typical interaction. The way in which the preexistent "blueprint" in the genome anticipates the construction of a new
organism corresponds completely to the first act of goal
setting, and the attainment of the goal, whereby strictly
causal sequences within the quite variable and adaptive choices
proffered by the milieu lead to the final realization of the
"blueprint," indubitably corresponds exactly to the postulated combined functions of Hartmann's three acts, if also
certainly on a level categorically lower than that of the conscious purposeful behavior of humans. Between these two
levels extends the continuous unmarkable scale of goal-
oriented behavior of animals and men, from aimless searching to the complex methodical procedures of humans.

The fact that the physiological ontogeny of any living
creature carries out a genuine goal-directed process — the
realization of a preexistent plan — leads all too easily to the
conviction that the same is true for the phylogenetic development, the evolution of that creature. In themselves the
words "development" and "evolution" seem to suggest this
interpretation. All of us have seen those wonderful sche-
matic charts of the evolutionary family tree of earthly organisms that show, at the bottom, the unicellular protozoa
and, as if struggling upward from these and other organisms,
the higher and still higher organisms until, finally, humans
are depicted at the top as the goal of all this effort and as
its crowning glory. Thus, having arrived, *finis!* Adjacent to
this charted phylogenesis that has, in fact, followed these

branching paths, a directional arrow is usually placed, *post festum,* which allows man to appear as if, from the very beginning, he had been the goal of the world of evolution — and humans are only too glad to be told such things.

Any attempt to interpret evolutionary developments in terms of intention and direction is just as misguided as the endeavors, undertaken by many scholars whose thinking is thoroughly scientific, to abstract laws from historical events that would permit predictions about the future course of history, somewhat in the way that knowing certain laws of physics enables possible predictions concerning physical events. That it should be possible for theoretical historiography to operate as scientifically as theoretical physics is an assumption not yet completely abandoned. Karl Popper has revealed the assumption to be a superstition: there is no doubt about human knowledge influencing the course of human history, but just as this accumulation of knowledge is unpredictable, so is the future course of history unpredictable. As Karl Popper demonstrates irrefutably in his book *The Poverty of Historicism,* no cognitive apparatus, be it a human brain or a computer, that is capable of making predictions can ever predict its own conclusions. All the attempts in this direction always produce a result only after the fact and thereby lose the characteristic feature of a prediction. "This argument, being purely logical," says Popper, "applies to scientific predictors of any complexity, including 'societies' of interacting predictors."

All of the above is as valid for the processes of phylogenesis as for the course of human history. Evolution is also decisively influenced by the acquisition of information, although its sort of unpredictability of acquisition is different from that of man's accumulation of knowledge. The minutest mutation signifying a gain of adaptive information changes the subsequent course of phylogenesis forever and irreversibly. For this reason the processes of becoming in the organic world, and from the very first appearance of life on earth, *cannot* in any way be fatefully predetermined. Rabbi Ben Akiba's famous aphorism that everything has already existed and everything has already happened is in direct opposition to historical truth: nothing extant has ever existed before; nothing that happens has happened before.

·◦}[TWO]{◦·

The Planlessness
of Evolution

THE CONCEPT OF TELEONOMY

When, as a comparative anatomist or as a comparative animal behaviorist, one becomes familiar with some particular segment of organic life, this familiarity can often involve one in a remarkable conflict. One is torn between admiring astonishment for the quite ingenious design features of some evolutionary constructs and disappointment concerning those solutions to problems, seeming obvious to our minds, which the processes of evolution have *not* found. So much that is clearly useless excess baggage is lugged along from generation to generation! Many scientists, among them Nicolai Hartmann, are inclined to overestimate degrees of usefulness and purposefulness. Hartmann does this when, for example, he expresses the belief that purposefulness is a priori insightful and has, thereby, the characteristic features of a category of the organic. He says: "It is quite obvious, that is, the essence of the matter is that an organism with purposeless organs, appendages, forms and functions cannot be viable." This statement definitely exaggerates the state of affairs; it must be brought into juxtaposition with Oskar Heinroth's repeatedly expressed recognition: "In organic life there is not only the useful but, as well, everything that is not *so* use*less* that it leads to the elimination of the species in question."

Nicolai Hartmann's statement, cited above, is even in itself not quite correct if one restricts it, as the philosopher does, "solely to the essential and relevant to life." The mistakes and dead ends into which evolutionary processes can be lured by momentary advantages are everything except irrelevant to the continued existence of the lineage in question. This problem was treated thoroughly in the first chapter of my book *Behind the Mirror*. The "purposefulness" of the anatomic characteristics as well as the behavior patterns of every living creature are oriented exclusively and demonstrably toward the propagation of the highest possible number of descendants, that is, toward the *survival* of the genome of the individual — and toward nothing else. The question, *For what purpose* does a cat have sharply pointed, curved claws? and the answer, For capturing mice, are shorthand for the single question, Which species-preserving capacities were provisionally pursued under the pressures of selection in order to have bred this kind of claw in cats? Questions about species-preserving purposefulness are identified as *teleonomic* questions in contradistinction to those teleological questions that query the meaning of life.

THE PURPOSELESS

In his publication "The Purposeless in Nature," Gustav Kramer brought together many examples of this phenomenon, but only one of them will be presented here: the air bladder of fishes with its functions for swimming that became an organ for breathing during the transition from aquatic life to terrestrial life. In the circulatory system of fishes, and already evident even among the early jawless cyclostomes (for example, lampreys), the heart and the gills are coupled in tandem, that is, all of the blood pumped from the heart must first pass directly to and then through the organ for breathing, the gills. This richly oxygenated blood, not mixed with venous blood, moves onward from the respiratory system into the body's circulatory system. But because the air bladder is an organ serviced by the body's circulatory system and has remained so even after having become a lung, that is, the sole organ for breathing for these terrestrial animals, and because the heart at this stage of development still has but one ventricle, the blood flowing into the body's circulatory system is mixed: partly oxygen-poor blood enters the ventricle from the body and partly oxygen-rich blood enters the ventricle from the lung. This most unsatisfactory solution, from a technical point of view, has been retained by all amphibians and by almost all reptiles. All of these animals are very rapidly fatigued — something that is seldom emphasized when they are spoken about as a group. A frog that has not reached some kind of cover after a certain number of leaps has to stop "to catch its breath" and remains exposed and is easily caught; the same is true for the most adroit and nimble lizard. No amphibian and no reptile is capable of the sustained muscular exertion that sharks or bony fishes or birds are capable of achieving.

Among the reptiles only crocodiles have a complete partition separating the right ventricle from the left ventricle and thereby separating the pulmonary or lung circuit from the systemic or body circuit. Crocodiles, however, are the descendants of a reptilian species that was probably bipedal and quite mobile, an ancestral form closely related in some respects to that of the birds. With crocodiles as the exception, only birds and mammals have pulmonary circuits and body circuits as completely separated loops in series: the lung veins carry the freshly aerated, pure arterial blood that flows into the heart's left ventricle and from there is pumped into the body's circulatory system, while the heart's right ventricle receives pure venous blood from the body circuit and pumps this into the lungs. Thus, in evolutionary time, it took from the first appearance of terrestrial vertebrates until the highest reptiles and the birds had come onto the scene for the "provisional construction" of a pulmonary circuit "shunted to" a body circuit to give way to a system having, once again, the functional efficiency of the circulatory system of the fishes, a systemic solution that had been sacrificed when gill breathing was abandoned.

FUNCTION CHANGE

Whether a genetically programmed structure or function is "purposeful" is a question that can never be correctly formulated except in terms of the unique constellation of environmental factors that always apply. Organs or organ parts that until just recently were of the greatest species-preserving value can become useless through just slight changes occurring in a creature's habitat. But also the changes initiated primarily by the organism itself, for example, the conquest of a new ecological niche, can neutralize the effectiveness of many structural and functional characteristics that, until the change, were species-preserving, or can even cause them to become harmful disadvantages. Fortunately for those researchers interested in evolutionary processes, "yesterday's adaptations" are dragged along with immense conservatism for quite some time. The no longer useful junk of physiological structures is then often re-employed in a way that is estranged from its original purpose, something that is customarily described as "function change."

The exploitation of the possibilities presented by yesterday's structures that have been lying around idle often appears to be nothing short of ingenious. A beautiful example is the conversion of the first gill cleft of primitive fishes into the external acoustic duct of frogs, reptiles, birds and mammals. When our predecessors made the transition from an aquatic life to a terrestrial life, from gill breathing to lung breathing, the gill clefts through which the water of life had flowed became functionless. The skeletal framework supporting the gill arch found partial use in the tongue-bone and in the larynx, but the gill slits themselves closed and disappeared — except for one: the foremost gill slit, the so-called spiracle that functions as the opening for inhalation among rays and many sharks, moved close alongside the semicircular canal and then beyond it to the organ for perceiving gravitation and acceleration. In a literal sense it was fitting and proper to bring this aperture, formerly conducting water, into connection with a structure already sensitive to vibrations, and to use it, filled now with air instead of water, as a "hearing tube" conducting sound waves.

A second, still more astounding example of function change is also connected with the formation of the ear. The temporomaxillary joint, the hinge of the jaw of fishes, amphibians, birds and reptiles, is formed by two bones, the *os quadratum,* which is rather firmly bound to the cranial skeleton, and the *os articulare,* which forms the hindmost part of the lower jaw. As mammals evolved from reptiles, the *os articulare* detached itself from the jaw and the *os quadratum* severed its firm connection to the base of the skull. The former bone came together with the tympanic membrane, the latter with the inner ear, and both became organs for transmitting sound waves, the so-called auditory ossicle. Simultaneously a new temporomaxillary joint, or jaw hinge, was formed farther forward. In this simultaneity lies a difficult mechanical problem since two joints, one in front of the other, on the same skeletal element must block each other's functioning.*

To a certain extent function change conceals the frequency with which organs lose their initial purposefulness, because a structure no longer used for its original function can almost always be used for some other purpose, somewhat in the way that a dust cloth or a cleaning rag can be made from an old piece of clothing. Even the vermiform appendix of humans serves as a source for lymphatic tissue (as well as, at one time, contributing to the "purposeful service of others," as my father chose to express it, in the support and sustenance of surgeons). What can evolve from an organ no longer in use is nearly unbelievable. A gill cleft becomes an ear, a jaw joint becomes an auditory ossicle, a parietal eye of ancient vertebrates becomes our pineal gland, an organ of internal secretion; and the endostyle, a filtering apparatus covered with cilia and a feeding groove of the very first vertebrate of all, becomes the thyroid gland — to cite just a few examples. Sometimes one has the anthropomorphic impression that an organ which has become functionless is given some kind of make-work to do, some purpose that, from the point of view of the organism as a whole, could actually be dispensed with, in the same way that an

---

*The transitions made from one joint to the other involved extremely complicated processes. An adequate explanation of how the mechanical problem was solved would demand a digression taking us further afield than we could want to go.

aged and no longer useful county or township official is given something, anything to do in charitable "recognition of services rendered." Actually it is natural that the presence of any unused tissue, in fact just the space taken up by an organ that has become useless, seems to present a selection advantage which "seduces" phylogenesis into making use of it as a "bargain-price opportunity" for some other purpose that would be much better served if, by anticipating that purpose, a newly created organ were formed from the ground up. But phylogenesis cannot look ahead, nor can an organism interrupt its life-sustaining functions for the period of time necessary for reconstructions, hanging out a sign saying "Closed for Renovations."

These processes, seen in all aspects of evolution, fundamentally illustrate the fact that an organism's overall construction is never comparable to an edifice planned by a farsighted human intellect for which, from the very beginning, all the necessary parts have been purposefully designed. An organism's architecture and interior furnishings are much more like the house of a homesteader who, in order to have some kind of shelter, first puts up a simple sod hut or log cabin and only later, when the number of people in his family and the extent of his prosperity have increased, builds and equips a larger house. The old hut or cabin is not torn down, however, but used as a storage shed or a stable or for some other purpose. Students of evolution can proceed in the same way an art historian studies an old cathedral — by analyzing the stages of construction and their history. But only rarely will the cultural historian discover that an alteration of those goals set at the beginning of a cathedral's construction is as drastic as that which the student of evolution must so often confront through his comparable researches.

ZIGZAG PATHS OF PHYLOGENESIS

The operational plans of humans are not immune to the sudden appearance of unanticipated circumstances that force already completed structures to be used for purposes completely different from those initially projected. Mansions have been turned into schools or old people's homes, passenger liners have been converted into hotels or military barracks. In evolutionary history, however, there are course changes to be found that signify an incomparably sharp deviation from a preceding adaptational direction pursued over a long period of time. Such abrupt changes of direction are sometimes clarifiable through "inventions" made in a particular habitat that enable the animals in question to colonize yet another and new ecological niche. An interesting "invention" in this category is the swim, or air, bladder of fishes. Its primary function was that of a breathing organ and was probably developed in swampy fresh water with a low and variable oxygen content. As was noted earlier, the air bladder was the prerequisite for a conquest of dry land by the predecessors of amphibians and reptiles. At the same time, however, as a hydrostatic organ it opened up the possibility among the fishes remaining behind to incorporate a solid bony skeleton whose weight, without the buoyancy of the air bladder, would have become, in the truest sense of the word, insupportable. In order to understand why the bony fishes and not the cartilaginous fishes (such as the sharks) populate the oceans in an overwhelming majority, one must have held a small shark and a bony fish of comparable size in one's own hands; only then is it possible to grasp the superiority of the physical strength, the effects of leverage, emerging from the bony fish's solid skeleton.

One of the most remarkable and most radical course

changes known to us in the history of higher animals is the return to the world's oceans undertaken by four-footed and land-dwelling reptiles and mammals. Here I am not thinking about the genesis of water-dwelling quadrupeds, such as sea turtles, crocodiles, seals and sea lions, that have retained the overall form of quadrupeds, but of those animals which, in body form and in the mechanics of their locomotion, became, once again, wholly fishlike — the Ichthyosauria among the reptiles and the whales among the mammals. The origins of the word "whale," from the Latin *squalus,* meaning a kind of sea fish, and the German word *Walfisch,* indicate that for a very long time man regarded these animals as fishes.

One must truly try to make present and vivid in one's mind the many phylogenetic steps that had to be taken for it to be possible for water-dwelling vertebrates to become land-dwelling vertebrates — how immense the journey must have been from fishes to mammals — in order fully to appreciate the stupendousness of an undertaking that once again would make a "fish" out of a mammal. If we could compare this phylogenetic feat to a human setting of personal goals, it might come close to the methods of production initiated by a technician who began to assemble an automobile and then, when the car was almost finished or even already completely assembled, made a motorboat out of it.

Understandably it was easier for reptiles than for mammals to achieve a fish's form and the fishlike movements necessary for aquatic locomotion. Most reptiles had, and still have today, a long and laterally flexible vertebral column that "snakes" noticeably when they move along on dry land; all of these forms swim "like fishes" when thrown into water. For a complete adaptation to this kind of locomotion it was necessary for reptiles only to evolve some vertical surfaces, most essentially a blade or fin on the propellant parts of the tail, as well as a resistance-minimizing, streamlined form for the body. When fishes "invented" such a caudal fin many millions of years earlier, most of them developed this blade, angling slightly upward, on the ventral side of their tail ends. The morphogenesis of the caudal fins of all bony fishes and the mature forms of these fins among sharks and sturgeons show to this day the same construction characteristic. The Ichthyosauria, however, "elected" a development of the opposite, upper side. A close inspection of the surviving reptiles adapted to swimming can make this choice appear understandable: among these forms the vertical ruddering surfaces of the tail are extended upward by means of cutaneous combs, raised scales and such other dermal projections, while the ventral surfaces — which usually drag along the ground when the creatures are crawling on land — remain flat. Probably this was the reason why the caudal fin of the Ichthyosauria grew on the top side of their tail ends.

For mammals the way back to a fish form was much farther; the mammalian vertebral column had, in the meantime, become shorter, the tail had thinned, and much of its musculature had been forfeited. When in motion now, the torso no longer waggled from side to side. Still remaining as a vestige of this former style of locomotion is the coordination of the leg movements during walking and trotting: during both of these gaits the back leg on one side moves at the same time as the front leg on the other side — just as this had arisen through the snaking torsos of ancient predecessors. When mammals swim — and almost all of them can — most of them also simply "walk" while in the water, using a fast pace, the locomotory coordination of which is not noticeably different from a fast walking pace executed on firm ground. Only intensely water-adapted forms such as otters, beavers and nutria paddle solely with the hind legs and paws when swimming forward languidly.

In addition to walking and trotting paces mammals are capable of another running movement coordination, the "gallop," which in differing but distinct variations from the simple support-sequence change, during which both fore-legs and both hind legs are moved simultaneously, to the complicated leg movements of hoofed animals, is almost always used as the *fastest* possible way to get from one place to another. The "slow gallop," usually described as "hop-ping," is a gait found among the hare species (Lagomorphae) and among the kangaroos. Among these animals the walking and trotting gaits have disappeared. Hares also use the two-legged leaping movement for swimming; they thrust them-selves through the water in lunges. Apparently no one has ever seen kangaroos swimming.

The shorter a mammal's appendages are, the more a gal-loping gait dominates over a trotting gait, and the slower a mammal's speed is, the more readily it falls into a gallop. What becomes so very beautifully apparent to the mind's eye when picturing a galloping dog is the important role the movement of the torso plays, specifically the arching and stretching out of the median vertical longitudinal plane (the sagittal plane) during this locomotory gait of the animal. The greatest advantage of galloping lies in being able to make use of the torso musculature for locomotion; these muscles are hardly used at all when walking and trotting.

The mammalian vertebral column, adapted to the various gaits, is more flexible in the vertical or perpendicular plane, and the musculature producing such movements is more strongly developed than the musculature for lateral or hor-izontal movements. When some mammals became aquatic animals once again and had to develop anew the snaking

movement so efficient for locomotion within a water me-
dium, the most natural thing for them was to take the currents and waves running vertically rather than horizontally.
In other words, the "undulatory" swimming of aquatic mammals is clearly derived from galloping. Following the same
principle, the propellant surfaces to be pushed against the
water had to be right-angled to the plane of movement and
thus be horizontal: the widened tail of some otters, the
paddle tail of beavers and the caudal fins of whales as well
as those of sea lions all form horizontal surfaces. Sea lions,
the so-called eared seals (Otariidae), also swim by "galloping" but not the seals (Phocidae): these mammals produce
lateral snaking movements with their hind ends and hind
legs; the surfaces of their propellant swimming feet are positioned vertically to the plane of movement.

Entire series of mammalian phyla took to the water. Among
the beasts of prey (Carnivora), those that are martenlike
(Mustelidae) appear to have been especially suited for this
because of the shortness and broadness of their legs and
because of the flexibility of their vertebral columns. For this
reason every imaginable sort of transitional musteline form
is to be found among them, from skunks and their near
relatives, the minks, which are very good divers, to the
otters, the sea otters and on to the South American giant
otter, which is similar to the genuine seal in so many aspects
that it is difficult to doubt the supposition that seals must
also have evolved from marten forms likewise adapted to
aquatic life. But against the acceptance of this assumption
is the evidence that eared seals (Otariidae) and seals (Phocidae) swim in different ways. This, in my opinion, forces
us to presume separate origins for these two groups. Among
both seal groups the tail, which among *otters* is finlike and
broadened and essential for "gallop" swimming, has been

reduced to a short stub. Among both the hind feet function as "tail fins"; they are positioned, however, as already stated, horizontally among the Otariidae and vertically among the Phocidae. This is what leads to the conclusion that Otariidae and Phocidae have most likely evolved independently of each other.

Among the sea cows (Sirenia) and the whales (Cetacea) the hind legs have disappeared entirely; a tail fin fabricated of skin and connective tissue is used for propulsion. Such a tail fin for mammals is a completely new organ evolved solely in the service of water adaptation. The sirenians are descended from mammals that at one time were closely related to the elephants and to the damans* and hyraxes (Hyracoidea).** Earlier the ancestral origin of whales was also attributed to this group, but more recently comparative anatomists have tended to place the predecessors of whales among carnivores, somewhere among the primitive marten forms. Supporting this classification is the fact that the whales — in contrast to the exclusively herbivorous sirenians — are almost exclusively carnivorous; only a few of the river dolphins consume some vegetable nourishment as well.

If one weighs the obvious disadvantages of constructions inherently attached to a creature that has already evolved into a warm-blooded, air-breathing, land-dwelling animal when, evolving further, it becomes once again a sea-dwelling animal, one wonders whether any of this can pay off. Such wonder is legitimate since every animal species and every plant species can be regarded as a "self-sustaining enter-

---

*A small, herbivorous, hoofed mammal (*Procavia syriaca*) of Palestine and Syria, the coney of the Old Testament.
**An order of Old World ungulate mammals that is now restricted to Africa and southwestern Asia and that comprises various extinct animals and the surviving hyraxes, which find their nearest living relatives in the elephants and sirenians but in many respects resemble rabbits.

prise." Because they often live in the polar regions, just maintaining body heat alone costs whales enormous amounts of energy, despite the thick layers of blubber that provide very efficient heat insulation and at the same time serve as a hydrostatic organ for increased floating capacity and round off contours for a streamlined form. Through these additional service functions the blubber loses its potential as stored energy since it may never be exploited and used. There is another reason why the nourishment of whales is not an entirely problem-free proposition: they must satisfy not only their energy requirements but also their water consumption through the animals they prey upon and eat. From dolphins kept in captivity it has been learned that if for some reason they refuse to eat, they die of thirst before they die of hunger, that is, they dehydrate before they starve. Another difficulty that has been partly compensated for through highly interesting special adaptations but that has never entirely been overcome is the necessity for whales to come to the surface of the water in order to breathe. Whales can, in fact, go without breathing for a very long time, but they drown extraordinarily easily if one attempts to capture them in nets — a theme on which everyone concerned with the capture, care and keeping of live whales at large modern oceanariums can weave many sad variations.

Giving birth also presents special difficulties. Whales and sea cows are the only mammals that never intentionally go on land and therefore must give birth while remaining in the water. That the newly born whale could drown is the most obvious danger, and female whales circumvent this latent disaster by means of immensely interesting instinctive behavior: another female whale, a friend of the bearing animal, very often her own mature daughter, stands by from the very beginning of the birth process ready to carry the baby whale, as soon as it emerges, up to the ocean's surface. To accomplish this the midwife whale balances the baby on her head, positioned there in such a way that its breathing spiracle, the so-called blowhole, can be lifted up and out of the water.

If one recalls and contemplates the many structural accommodations and behavioral improvisations by means of which difficulties have been overcome and problems solved — difficulties and problems associated directly with revamping a land-dwelling mammal into one that has become a water-dweller — one is amazed (as so often) by the ingeniousness of the "well-thought-through" measures and the supplementary inventions; on the other hand, one cannot avoid being astonished that such an incisive change in the direction of adaptation can pay off at all, or, expressed in another way, that the water mammal can manage to hold its own in competition with the water-dwelling "naturals," the fishes.

BLIND ALLEYS OF EVOLUTION

The route taken by evolution is quite apparently determined by that kind of accident which rewards with a selection advantage a particular genetic change occurring in just as particular environmental conditions prevalent at the time. How often this route can change direction has been sketched in the previous section. These direction changes leave behind traces in the form of "yesterday's adaptations" (discussed on page 23) still to be found within the structures of the creatures involved, allowing the researcher concerned with evolution to reconstruct the stages of development. The genome itself contains the outcome of a vast number of mutations and selection processes; yet it does not embody any kind of "record" of the sequences of these occurrences. Because each individual mutation is contingent upon chance and proceeds nondirectionally, the improbability that evolution could ever return along the exact same route it has come is expressible only in astronomical numbers. This obvious fact of no return, evident to us now because of our current knowledge concerning genetic and phylogenetic processes, was conceptualized many years ago by the Belgian paleontologist Louis Dollo, on the basis of his comparative phylogenetic studies and formulated in the law of the "irreversibility of adaptation."

The more specialized an adaptation is — in other words, the greater the length and the more meandering the route of sequential mutational and selective processes that has led to the present state of a species — that much more improbable it is that the adaptation can be reversed. Whenever a selection pressure appears that could make a reversal advantageous, evolution goes almost invariably along a path other than the one along which it came. When, for example, one group of fishes that through adaptation to life at the deepest ocean levels has reduced the hydrostatic function of the air (swim) bladder and thereby become much heavier than water and no longer capable of floating, for some reason begins to generate forms that swim freely, the now vestigial air bladder will not be fetched from the attic storeroom. Instead, a new apparatus for floating, in the shape of wings or hydrofoils, is "invented," most often fashioned from the pectoral fins, as among the Triglidae and among the Dactylopteridae (the flying gurnards), to which, just because of these winglike pectoral fins, the capacity for flight was, for a long time, erroneously attributed.

Another and even more beautiful example of the process here being discussed has been cited by O. Abel in his textbook on paleozoology. The heavy armor of tortoises and turtles developed first among terrestrial forms through a broadening of the ribs and of the spinous processes of the vertebrae that fused, finally, into a closed shell. The group conquered the open seas, probably on the way through sweetwater swamps, and there the heavy armor of the terrestrial predecessors was made lighter by means of breach formations (fontanels), which first began to appear at the outer edges of the carapace and later progressed inward toward the vertebral column; in the same way, retrograde developments also appeared in the abdominal armor. Thus open sea forms eventually evolved with very light and, in the interests of a streamlined shape, only very shallowly vaulted shells. From such kinds of highly specialized seagoing turtles, during the early Tertiary period, some forms branched off that returned to a life in coastal regions where possessing a strong armor was again an advantage. Over what still remained of the old osseous armor a new armor now molded itself, consisting of small, irregular, mosaiclike polygonal plates pressing against one another. The descendants of these sea turtles that had subsequently, secondarily become coast dwellers, such as the Psephophorus extant from the Eocene epoch through the Pliocene epoch, then became, still again, seagoing animals among whom the reduction of the bony armor was repeated once more. In this way is explained, on the basis of available fossil forms, the otherwise completely inexplicable fact that the leatherback turtle living today in the open seas carries two armored shells, one lying over the other, both of which are retrogressive and both of which are not functionally efficient.

In a certain sense, becoming highly specialized is always, in the long run, dangerous for every creature doing this. Not only is it most improbable that the "way back" can be found; as specialization increases, the possibility decreases that any new and different route can be found at all, should the route one is on turn out to be a blind alley. The number of possibilities for useful applications of every construct, including any tool devised by humans, decreases with its specialization.

The further a special adaptation is pushed, that much less is it capable of adjusting to any change occurring in that to which it has become adapted. Swallows and swifts are adapted in an admirable way to the capture of flying insects; the species of these groups are successful and are spread in large numbers throughout the northern Temperate Zone. Among no other bird species do we know of such annihilating catastrophes as those befalling these flocks when, through sudden and early onsets of adverse autumnal weather, the insect flights cease before the birds have started their fall migration.

Phylogenerically specialized adaptation is comparable to a commercial venture in which large sums of capital are invested for manufacturing a new article before it is known how long an upward market trend for the sale of the product will hold. The more specialized the factory facilities and equipment are, that much less is the possibility that they can be used to produce something else after the boom has ceased. What can induce species mutation just as what can induce any human venture into the most inapt specialized adaptations is the prospect of an initial huge profit. Positive feedback in the form of capital gains and of information increments, discussed in my book *Behind the Mirror,* is pursued by phylogenesis without any insightful prescience of the inevitable consequences, and by human industrial enterprises despite some prescience.*

*See also *Civilized Man's Eight Deadly Sins:* "Every cycle with a positive feedback leads sooner or later to catastrophe" (p. 29).

THE EFFECTS OF INTRASPECIFIC COMPETITION

Natural selection does not give any preference at all to anything that, in the long run, could be advantageous for the species but blindly rewards everything that, momentarily, affords greater procreative success. This blindness appears with special clarity in those cases where this success is not dependent on circumstances related to extraspecific environmental factors but, instead, on the interactions among conspecifics. Intraspecific rivalry and competition can result in bizarre formations that interpose impediments to the best interests of the species concerned. Among those species in which the choice of a mating partner rests with the female, as among very many birds whose precopulation courting displays are carried out collectively, and also among higher mammals, a result is the development of display organs selected exclusively for their appeal to the innate releasing mechanisms of the females. The competition among the males is then reduced, virtually exclusively, to an exhibition of the most effective "advertising technique." This appears particularly inane when, for enhancement as effective signal structures, organs are enlisted that serve another function which is thereby impaired through this enhancing differentiation. For example, a male Argus pheasant's secondary feathers, exaggeratedly elongated and embellished with exceedingly beautiful eyelike spots of color that look as if they had been painted on, are such a structure. Fully grown Argus cocks are still capable of flying, but their capacities for flight are also clearly impeded. Enhanced development of the secondary feathers must achieve some kind of compromise between the demands made by the cock's need to be able to fly and those made by the "taste" of Argus hens: if the bird cannot fly very well, a ground predator will kill him before he can produce any offspring; if his secondary feathers are not impressive enough, he will also remain without progeny because the female will have preferred some other cock.

Another example of a wrong track down which intraspecific selection has led an animal species is taken from a group of mammals, the deer. Among the large genera and species of this group the males always carry impressive sets of antlers consisting of a bony substance. Every year the antlers are sloughed off and grown anew. One must try to imagine what sorts of disadvantages this phenomenon means for these species. It is very costly, in terms of energy, to have to grow every year a heavy tree of bone often weighing many pounds. As long as they are growing, the antlers are covered with a haired skin, the "velvet," and are extraordinarily vulnerable and must, among those species living within thick forests, hamper movement considerably — however precisely the deer are oriented to the overall dimensions of the projecting surroyal, or crown, points, and however cleverly they know how to maneuver with these branches. All of this is selected for because the antlers serve in rival and ritual fighting for territorial rights during the few weeks of the rutting season and, in addition, because they are required by the females as optical releasers. A. B. Bubenik has demonstrated that with an artificial and exaggeratedly large set of deer antlers a man can entice away the entire harem of the strongest local buck.

What is selected for is simply whatever, at the moment and under the prevailing circumstances, promises the highest number of progeny and not whatever would, in the long run, serve species preservation and, in this sense, be teleonomic.

Among those characteristics and behavior patterns selected that are advantageous only to the genome of an individual and are senseless and inappropriate for the preservation of the species as a whole belongs the infanticide observed in troops of langur monkeys (Semnopithecinae) and in prides of lions. Within both species a male possesses a harem of several females. When a reigning pasha must yield to another, the new sovereign bites dead all those offspring still in the care of their mothers. This means a propagation advantage for him since the mothers, deprived of their offspring, come into estrus earlier than those allowed to rear their young and can be covered by him. What happens to those offspring born after the former pasha has yielded to a successor appears not to be known. Some observers, among them Y. Sugiyama, who have written accounts of the infanticide practiced by langur monkeys regard the phenomenon as pathological and exceptional, which, with regard to the infrequency of its appearance, is not entirely improbable.

Those functions of selection discussed in this section that are clearly detrimental to the preservation of the species constitute, in my opinion, a strong argument for the assumption that the evolutionary process incorporates no integral plan leading to a development in the direction of a greater completeness of adaptation and still less effecting a developmental tendency "upward."

Adaptation to a specific given — circumstance or condition — can be equated with acquisition of information about that given. Intraspecific selection promotes information only about the characteristics of the contenders involved in the competition. Through intraspecific selection the species "experiences" nothing about the external world and thereby, relative to that world, stumbles extremely easily into the most unteleonomic blind alleys of evolution.

RETROGRADE EVOLUTION, OR "SACCULINISATION"

In the preceding sections I hope to have shown sufficiently that from each already achieved stage of development evolution can go on in any direction whatever, blindly responding to every new selection pressure that turns up. We need to be aware that within the terminology just used, in "direction" of evolution, an initially inadvertent value judgment is implicit. This will be discussed in the second part of the book. For the present context it is quite enough if every one of us understands what is meant when speaking about a higher or a lower living being. When we use the terms "higher" and "lower" in reference to living creatures and to cultures alike, our evaluation refers directly to the amount of information, of knowledge, conscious or unconscious, inherent in these living systems, irrespective of whether it has been acquired by natural selection, by learning or by exploratory investigation, and irrespective of whether it is preserved in the genome, in the individual's memory or in the tradition of a culture.

Now, in this section, an evolutionary process will be discussed the direction of which appears to lead to a value diminution. It is nearly impossible to find an immediately understandable expression for this process. The words "involution," "decadence" or even "degeneration" all have implications not applicable to the process referred to here. "Retrograde evolution" is perhaps the best expression. This process is so specific that I was tempted to call it "Sacculinisation" after an impressive example. As a word, "Sacculinisation" is unambiguous but in need of a definition; I coined it by taking the name of a creature in which the process of retrograde evolution is especially vivid. The crayfish *Sacculina carcini* is probably a descendant of the large phylum of copepod shrimps (Copepoda), perhaps also of the goose barnacles (Cirripedia). As a larva freshly emerged from an egg, this crayfish is a typical nauplius, that is, a little six-footed crustacean that paddles swiftly through the water and is equipped with a central nervous system whose programming allows it forthwith to search out its prospective host, the common green crab (*Carcinides maenas*), and straightway to fasten itself firmly onto, then to bore into the host's underside at the boundary between the cephalothorax, the united head and thorax, and the tail. As soon as this has been accomplished, simple unstructured tubes grow out of the front end of the litle crayfish into the body of the host, which they penetrate throughout, just as the mycelium, the mass of interwoven threadlike filaments of a mushroom, penetrates its nutrient substratum. The eyes, the extremities and the nerve system of the crayfish-parasite disappear completely; it grows on the outer side of the host into a gigantic genital gland that, on larger crabs, can reach the size of a cherry.

Analogous manifestations are found among many parasites and as well in many animal species that do not function as pests at all, such as the so-called symbionts, which are decidedly useful to their animal hosts. Symbionts that show evidence of retrograde evolution include, for example, very many of our household animals, our pets and our farm animals, which have gradually forfeited all of those specialized adaptations that were indispensable to their ancestors for independent survival in the wild. Compared to their undomesticated ancestors, almost all domesticated animals have lost much of their freedom of movement; all of them have gained only in respect to those attributes useful to humans and for which man has consciously or unconsciously exerted selection pressure. Customarily one calls these processes of becoming "house animals" domestication. Our aesthetic sensibilities assess most of the external aspects of domestication negatively. Julian Huxley spoke of vulgarization.

In fact, in comparison, most of the undomesticated ancestral forms of our household animals appear decidedly "noble" — but there are at least two telling exceptions. In lectures on this subject I have enjoyed showing illustrations of wild forms and domesticated forms, the one following the other, and then abruptly showing, in reverse order, a purebred Arabian horse and Przewalski's wild horse. When this is done, even those familiar with the subject take several seconds to sort out the sequence, to realize that the Arabian is the domesticated form of Przewalski's horse. What is true for the horse with regard to aesthetics is true for the dog with regard to social behavior patterns. Beginning about fourteen thousand years ago, man has continuously exerted exacting selection pressure on an already highly social wild form and particularly on the development of those attributes regarded as human virtues: the capacities for love and for fidelity, courage and fortitude, bravery and obedience. No wonder then that within this span of time, creatures have developed that excel us in all these qualities.

The evolutionary processes occurring among parasites and among symbionts always have, as a prerequisite, a partnership involvement with another living organism that takes over all those functions that have retrogressed and been lost by the sponging parasite or symbiont partner. The common green crab forages for food, moves away from danger into a safe place and performs innumerable other functions while the parasite allows itself to rely on the host to take over all of these responsibilities. Domesticated animals are, in the same way, dependent upon and subject to human functions.

Whether or not a species can fall victim to retrograde

evolution without another living form — host or symbiont — carrying out vicariously the necessary survival functions is a very important question. Only a single certain
example is known for manifestations of domestication in an
independent, free and certainly not parasitic animal — the
cave bear. The specifics of what I mean by the manifestations
of domestication are set forth in chapter 5; what engages us
here is that, through his examination of cave-bear skeletons
excavated from the Dragon Caves near Mixnitz in Styria,
Austria, Wilhelm von Marinelli found clear indications of
domestication such as are not known in the entire animal
kingdom except among domestic animals, particularly the
domestic dog. Some of the cave-bear skulls had structures
reminiscent of bulldog skulls while others showed the be-
ginnings of the mutations characteristic of extremely long-
snouted dogs, such as collies and greyhounds. Both types
of skull structure were found in association with correlated
abnormalities in the structure of the leg skeleton. The cave
bear has become known as the predominant fossil for those
geological strata in which it is found; during its time of
predominance it was the largest and mightiest animal within
the territory it chose to occupy. What is also now certain is
that no still larger beast of prey existed that ate cave bears.

This is the only indication we have that signs of retrograde
evolution can also appear when no host or symbiont partner
compensates for diminished capacities. The question of retrograde evolution and the indications cited are of such vital
importance for us humans because our species has already
begun to show, as far as our bodies are concerned, unmistakable manifestations of domestication, and because a re-
trogression of specific human characteristics and capacities
conjures up the terrifying specter of the less than human,
even of the inhuman. If one judges the adapted forms of

the parasites according to the amounts of retrogressed information, one finds a loss of information that coincides with and completely confirms the low estimation we have of them and how we feel about them. The mature *Sacculina carcini* has no information about any of the particularities and singularities of its habitat; the only thing it knows anything about is its host.

·⊰[THREE]⊱··

Creative Evolution

ADAPTATION AS A COGNITIVE PROCESS

Today we know, through the findings of Manfred Eigen and Ruthild Winkler, that the origin of life was not at all an event of such colossal improbability all nonvitalistic biologists and philosophers once assumed it to be. Rupert Riedl has also convincingly demonstrated in his book *The Strategy of Genesis* that chance is circumscribed in multifarious ways: through the successful advantages it achieves in some cases and also, above all, through the complex interactions among the genes — which never go into action independently of one another, as was once thought to be the case.

We are still convinced, as we always have been, that it is very improbable that genetic change, in itself, can improve the survival chances of an organism, yet this improbability confronts the realization that if such a genetic change opens up new possibilities for the organism's increased command over its environment, then a change can prove to be commensurately worthwhile. Every mutation through a new combination of genetic factors that provides the organism with a new opportunity for coming to terms with the conditions of its environment signifies no more and no less than that *new information about this environment* has got into that organic system. *Adaptation is essentially a cognitive process.* This insight helps us to understand that intraspecific selection instigates no adaptation whatsoever; the apprehended data fed into the organism as a result of intraspecific selection relate in no way to that organism's environment; these data refer exclusively to the attributes of that organism's species.

The material that selection engages always comprises the characteristics of the phenotype; these phenotypic characteristics result from purely accidental alterations or new combinations of hereditary factors as well as, naturally, modifications. It is formally correct to assert that evolution proceeds according to the principles of chance and elimination. This assertion appears to be implausible, however, because the few billion years our planet has existed could not have provided sufficient time for the genesis of higher living beings and of humans from the viruslike predecessors of all living organisms to have been possible in just this way. Yet we know through the findings of Eigen and Winkler that the potential effects of chance are "curbed" and channeled, on the one hand, through the chemical compositions of the elements and, on the other hand, through the complex interactions among the genes, which, as Rupert Riedl has shown, are never independently active.

Still, our view remains unchanged and, as before, regards a mutation through which the survival chances of a species can be improved as highly improbable. But against this improbability must be ranged the just as potent improvement in the chances of survival, and for propagation, that emerge as a result of each auspicious genetic change. The increment of knowledge that is associated with and invested in each new adaptation bears interest and provides a further "gain in capital" through the subsequent increase in the number of surviving progeny. With this increased number the probability also increases that one of these descendants will be the one into whose lap the next mutation "jackpot" will fall. There exists, thus, for all living beings, a relationship of positive feedback between an acquisition of knowledge and capital gains — the more you have the more favorable are the circumstances for getting even more. Perhaps this effective sphere of cyclic activity can be made concrete and comprehensible through a comparison with commercial undertakings. A large chemical concern regularly invests a considerable part of its net profits in its laboratories on the justifiable assumption that the acquisition and accumulation of knowledge so achieved will more than pay for itself through further capital gains. (Strictly speaking, this is not a comparison of similar or like things at all but the description of a special case; industrial enterprises are also living systems.)

An "adaptation to" a given environment always signifies, therefore, the creation of a correspondence that, in a certain sense, is an *image* of this environment. Donald MacKay speaks in this case about *representational information* (a concept that is in no way identical to that of the information theorist or cybernetician) "built up" or formed within the living system "from the descriptive content of the external material world." From the simplest molecular adaptations of the earliest viruslike predecessors of living organisms, to the scientific world view accepted by thinking, reflecting humans, flows a gapless, complete, uninterrupted series of transitional image sequences.

This evolutionary progression is, however, not identical with the process I would like to conceptualize as creative evolution. I have so carefully described the wild zigzag paths of evolution in such circumstantial detail only because those paths show so unmistakably that a predetermined direction is *not* incorporated as part of the inner being of organic life. That example of the many-branched river delta often cited as illustrative of evolutionary processes does not apply in one instance: while all the waterways shown always run forward downhill, the direction of the evolutionary processes within some branches of phylum life can reverse and retrogress. One can even say about the viruses that their genesis has led living matter back to states of nonliving matter.

But most important, it must be clear to us that a better and more assured state of adaptation of a creature to its environment, together with its degree of differentiation and the duration and complication of its evolutionary history, *may not be equated with the level* — the "highness" or "lowness" — *of its development.* A paramecium is just as well adapted to the particularities of the environment occupied by its species as man is to his. If one were to weigh the relative chances for survival of the one species against those of the other during the immediate future on our earth, the outlook for the "lower" form of life would, in fact, appear to be decidedly better. The nearness to perfection of adaptation is of little use in a definition of the "higher"; this also applies to the degree of organic complexity as well as to the degree of differentiation and the extent of subordination of parts within an entire systemic whole. What one could, at best, take as a measure of the "higher" in organic development is the volume of information that has been acquired and stored.

"MOVING ON UP A LITTLE HIGHER"

The path of development taken by a living system depends upon both external and internal chance occurrences: everything that happens in our world, to cite Manfred Eigen and Ruthild Winkler, "resembles a vast game in which nothing is determined in advance but the rules." Although in principle not purpose-oriented, evolution is a cognitive process. Our insight into the absence of any predetermination may not, as a consequence, be permitted to exclude us from the acknowledgment of one fact: the creatures most eminent during each of the designated geologic epochs of the earth's history are without exception "higher" animals than those of preceding epochs. We would have to violate our sense of values if we were to doubt that the sharks and aquatic vertebrates of the Devonian period were not higher living beings than the trilobites of the Cambrian, that the batrachian reptiles of the Carboniferous period were not higher than the sharks, and that the reptiles of the Mesozoic era were not higher than the amphibians of the Paleozoic era.

This nonrational assessment indubitably reflects something actually extant in our external world, and this actuality demands an explanation that, initially, we are able to present only in the form of a rather uncertain hypothesis. Adaptation, in itself, is only a cognitive and not a creative process, yet not only the object of cognition — what "is to be known" — but also the comprehending, knowing subject has in the course of epochal time become increasingly complicated. The game that engages everything with everything else is played not only between living systems and the inorganic environment but also among the innumerable species of extant living systems, and the character of this game is not at all always and everywhere a struggle for existence but just as often, and above all when a grand series of bold moves are being made on the board, a concerted action, a symbiosis. An ecological system is an exceedingly complicated construct with innumerable abetting as well as inhibiting interactions. Our hypothesis intends to imply that it is this game of multifarious organismic interplay that permits evolution to be creative. It is not a principle that is all-embracing, but one that applies to the reciprocal influences exerted by closely related and often similar forms, influences that lead to "innovations" and "inventions" which have never, ever, existed before.

An example taken from mechanics can show us that the selection pressure leading to a greater differentiation and to the further complication of a system is exerted primarily by other closely related systems. Henry Ford's first product to achieve international renown, the so-called tin Lizzie, celebrated a striking success in competition with horse-drawn conveyances. Users of Ford's automobile were satisfied with the two-gear plate unit of the drive mechanism, which required the application of a strong sustained pressure on one pedal for as long as the first gear was supposed to remain in function. (The widespread satisfaction was expressed in the well-known saying of a pious grandmother: "If God had intended the Ford car to have a three-speed gear, He would have fitted it with one.") It was not any horse-drawn vehicle that later forced Ford to design and incorporate a multiple-gear unit but the competition from other automobile manufacturers.

An argument for the assumption that the game engaging everything with everything else, as it is played out among the multitudes of coexisting living systems, is a significant factor for impelling evolution "onward and upward" and for admitting its creativity lies in the fact that the phylogenetic development of individual living systems comes close to a complete standstill when such encounters with similar systems cease to take place. This happens most often in isolated ecological niches; "living fossils" from the lower levels of the oceans are particularly well known. Coming not from those deep ocean levels but still an especially impressive example is the sweetwater crustacean *Triops cancriformis,* belonging to the phyllopoda. It has secured for itself a truly unusual, out of the way ecological niche in the pools and ponds that form for only a short time, and by no means every year, in the flood-overrun regions adjacent to large rivers. During the intervals between inundations the members of this species survive as eggs that are impervious to damage by drought or by frost. This crustacean can be found in the pools of the river-flooded meadows near my father's house in Altenberg on the Danube River not far outside Vienna. Thanks to an early-awakened passion for maintaining aquaria that coincided with a growing special interest in phyllopod crustaceans, I can report with certainty that *Triops cancriformis* turned up on our territory in the year 1909, showed itself next in 1937, and then appeared again in 1949 (between the years 1940 and 1949 lies an observational void produced by the war). The important fact for us here is that this species has been traced back to and authenticated as extant during the middle Triassic period. Not only that, the well-preserved fossil impressions taken from those geologic strata show the crustacean as having the same filter apparatus, the same leaflike swimming appendages that serve as gills with the fissures formed by pinnated bristles, that someone will see when the river floods once again, making it quite certain that the Triassic crustaceans and those of tomorrow both belong to the same species and not just to the same genus.

What, in the course of time, urges "upward" might be the simple circumstance that, in the course of evolution, every organism variant has had somehow to achieve access to a new ecological niche, for the very homely reason that everywhere "below" has already been fully "occupied." Similar circumstances appear to prevail when an organism is capable of mastering two differing functional adaptations, meaning that it could also, to a certain extent, occupy two ecological habitats. This is certainly the case when a living system has at its disposal a number of forms of behavior each of which must be brought into use within a quite specific environmental situation. In such cases a higher "command post" or control center is necessary that is capable of placing several potentially possible behavior patterns under total restraint in order to release from inhibition the one particular form of behavior that, for the situation prevailing at the moment, is the most adequate. The everyday expressions, "deciding" to do something and "making up" one's mind, designate an analogous process at a higher level. But, as Erich von Holst demonstrated with the earthworm, just this inhibiting-releasing function is the most primal and most important achievement of a brainlike organization, such as the supraesophageal ganglion of earthworms and other annelids. This "command post" keeps in continuous repressive check the constantly proffered movement patterns coming from the endogenous stimulus production of the animal and gives free rein only to those patterns that, under the momentarily prevailing circumstances, can deploy their species-preserving actions. The command post is informed by the sensory organs about which particular environmental situation is prevalent at the time, and it possesses genetically programmed information about which of the movement patterns that are available and standing ready fits which environmental situation. The more finely differentiated the behavior possibilities are that an animal has at its disposal, that much more versatile and complex will the performances be that the central control organ demands from what, as it were, it governs.

We are already well acquainted with those animals, such as starfishes and some snails, that, on a rather simple level, can orient themselves and find their way quite well within spatially complicated surroundings. They are capable of accustoming themselves to habitual routes and are able to find the way back to those places they usually occupy after having completed quite complicated feeding tours. Among some limpets (*Patella*) the growth of the animal's shell conforms to the particular contours of the place the limpet occupies and from which, no matter the amount of force exerted, it cannot be dislodged. Here the special teleonomic value of being able to find the way back becomes spectacularly apparent. Other simple animals have the advantageous faculty of swimming through the water with incredible swiftness: the arrowworms (Chaetognatha) are, relative to their own length, probably the fastest free-swimming animals that there are. But arrowworms cannot come to grips and cope with the stationary obstacles that circumscribe their swimming channels.

Were we, however, to search now for animals that are capable of mastering complex spatial structures through learning as well as being able to swim at lightninglike speeds, then we must move on up to a very much higher level of living system, up to certain spinous dorsal-finned fishes. These forms are the ones that, through spatial learning, have complete command of channels in the spatially richly structured biotope of coral reefs. The drilled mastering of channels is acquired by these fishes through exploratory behavior.

Territorial fishes "know" from every possible point within their ranges the shortest route to secure cover. The development level of these fishes is astonishingly high; they surprise one again and again by their curiosity and by their "unfishlike" intelligence.

CULTURAL EVOLUTION

From the recorded histories of civilizations we know that the directions taken during the evolution of cultures can change and follow zigzag routes analogous to those taken during the genetic evolution of animal and plant species. A further fact about which we are certain is that cultural evolution — the psychosocial, as Julian Huxley has termed it — develops many times faster than the phylogenetic. In my book *Behind the Mirror,* I attempted to establish a natural theory of knowledge hypothesizing that the conceptual thinking of humans came into being through an integration of several already preexistent cognitive capacities. The first of these several capacities to be recalled here is that of spatial orientation and conceptualization. The comprehended forms of space and time are, in my opinion, really only one form, and that is the eidetic form of movement in space and time.

The second most important capacity that, together with the comprehension of space, made possible the new systemic function of conceptual thinking is the abstracting capacity of Gestalt perception without which we could not grasp the constancies of objects. And a third capacity is that of exploratory behavior with its apposite, practical interest in objects. Surely the practical exploration of environmental entities is what led an individual being on the threshold of becoming human to discover the verifiable fact that his reaching, touching, seizing and holding hand was as much an object of the same real external world as were the other objects being explored. At this moment the first connection was completed that bridged the abyss between apprehending and comprehending.

Noam Chomsky believes that conceptual thinking came into being through the services it rendered in mastering aspects of the extraspecific environment and only secondarily attained an association with speech. There are certainly compelling arguments for this assumption, but despite them I still believe that conceptual thinking and language originated hand in hand, for just as soon as an approach was opened to conceptualizations, it was inevitable that concepts for them would be found.

The geneses of conceptual thinking and verbal language had unforeseeable biological consequences. Since the discovery of evolution there have been many discussions among biologists whether acquired characteristics are or are not heritable. Many years ago I devised a sarcastic aphorism that expressed the following principle: "A researcher often first becomes aware that something does *not* usually *occur* when an exceptional case shows him what it would look like *if it* occurred regularly." The newly combined and brought into being, the never-there-before conceptual thinking of humans, makes the inheritance of (naturally not genetically) acquired characteristics possible. When someone invents the bow and arrow, at first he and his family and their tribe have it, but soon thereafter all of mankind has it, and the probability that the invention will be forgotten again is not greater than the possibility that an organ of the body, of comparable importance, will become vestigial. The colossal capacity for adaptation accrued in human beings who find it possible to carry on in the most diversified environments imaginable is an enunciation of the extreme rapidity with which cultural evolution proceeds.

A second, perhaps still more essential consequence of conceptual thinking and of verbal language is the ties by which these bind individuals to one another. The rapid dissemination of knowledge and the assimilation of opinions, beliefs and convictions by all members of a social group produce a unity of consensus and confraternity such as has never existed before. Bonds of this sort entwine larger and smaller clusters of human beings. Commonly shared knowledge, skills and aspirations produce cultural unity. Mind is for me just these basic accomplishments of human society brought about through conceptual thinking, verbal language and shared tradition. The life of the mind is a consequence of a *social* effect. I have often maintained that a human, taken alone, is no human at all; only as a member of a reasoning group can a person be completely human. The life of the mind is fundamentally supraindividual life; the individual's concrete realization of reasoning communality is what we call culture.

CULTURE AS A LIVING SYSTEM

However great the gulf — Nicolai Hartmann would say the "hiatus" — between a purely genetic evolution and the emergence and development of a culture may appear to be, both still remain subject to the fundamental rules applicable to the game of becoming. The assumption that the development of a culture is governed by insight and reasoned knowledge and pursues with prudent certitude that chosen path toward the "higher" is an erroneous assumption. None of the basic cognitive functions not yet specifically human — perception of depth and direction, a central-nervous representation of space, Gestalt perception and the capacity for abstraction, insight and learning, voluntary movement, curiosity and explorative behavior, imitation — is, through its integration for conceptual thinking, made dispensable; none loses even the least part of its significance. Among humans all of these functions are more strongly developed than any of them is among an animal species, even when they represent for those animals a fulfillment of the most vital, life-furthering functions. Behavior motivated by curiosity is the most important activity of the rat, and the rat's survival depends on it — but humans have even more curiosity. Accurate optic perception of complexly shaped entireties and formed units is one of the most important accomplishments of certain birds — but humans are better at this than birds are, and so on.

The human mind is dependent upon these primary accomplishments and basic functions but is even more dependent upon the equilibrium of their interplay — a balance that can be more easily disturbed than the indispensable partial function of each of the single capacities alone. A bit too much of one of these, not quite enough of another, means a malfunction of the whole, signifies a sickness of the mind. But this would, of necessity, using the social concept of mind as I have defined it, also denote an epidemic disease.

The history of mankind pitilessly imparts to us the information that cultures, just as all other living systems, can debilitate and disintegrate. Comparative studies such as those contrived by Oswald Spengler, for example, inform us that our own culture is standing at the edge of its grave. As I stated in chapter 1, Oswald Spengler was exactly what Karl Popper calls a "historicist"; Spengler believed that the senescence and dissolution of high cultures could be predicted logically, that is, could be accounted for on the basis of a "logic of time" and as a "natural aging of all cultures."

Nothing is more foreign to the evolutionary epistemologist and, as well, to the physician than the doctrine of fatalism. For this reason I feel obligated to search for the causes of degeneration in our culture and, as far as they are discernible and identifiable, to recommend countermeasures. In *Behind the Mirror,* in the chapter bearing the same heading as that of this section, I attempted to demonstrate the number of ways and at how many points the development of a culture is analogous to that of an animal and a plant species. The developmental processes are enacted on quite dissimilar levels of integration; yet both systems, cultures and species, are "enterprises based on reciprocal feedback between the acquisition of power and the acquisition of knowledge."

The analogies between the two different kinds of development extend so far that analogous methodologies for their study have, as a result, ensued. The history of culture and especially the historical approach to linguistic research utilize the same methodology as that employed in phylogenetic research by the comparative morphologist; from the similarities and dissimilarities of current living systems (or contemporary words), origins or derivations are traced and reconstructions are made of common ancestral forms. Up to the latter part of the last century philosophers of history attempted to cling to the theory of a single, unitary development encompassing the history of all mankind. Then Arnold Toynbee and others pointed out that the development of human civilizations presents us with a "tree of decisions" that is just as branched and irregular as the "family tree of all living things" shown in my textbook *The Foundations of Ethology.*

As far as my knowledge extends, Erik Erikson was the first person to draw attention to the parallels between the branching of the tree of species life and the historical development of cultures. He coined the apt expression "pseudo-speciation" for the divergent development of different cultures from the same source. Culture groups behave toward one another in many respects as do different but very closely related animal species. The close relationship must be emphasized because in no known case have two human cultures diverged so extensively from each other that they could coexist within the same ecological domain without competing — as, for example, two closely related duck species, shovelers and mallards, can without any difficulty at all. In *Behind the Mirror,* in the sections on cultural-historical ritual formation and on cultural invariance, I have discussed the very real human accomplishments that contribute to distinctiveness among cultural groups and constitute them as units.

INHERITANCE AND VARIABILITY IN CULTURE

When inheritance is mentioned nowadays, one is so accustomed to thinking in terms of the genetic, that is, in terms of the biological process, of phylogenetically received information being passed on to descendants, that one tends to forget the original, legal meaning of the word "inheritance." Recalling this meaning is necessary, however, because nascent culture requires the stable transmission of certain behavior norms that become traditional, and, although these traditional norms are never fixed genetically, they play a role in culture very similar to that of the stable transmission of genetic information in phylogenesis. Moreover, deviations from these norms within a culture are just as indispensable for the continued development of that culture as variabilities within the genotype are for phylogenesis.

The ritualized norms of social behavior that are passed on to us through the traditions of our cultures represent a complicated supporting "skeleton" of human society without which no culture would be able to subsist. Like all other skeletal elements, those of culture can also carry out their supporting function only at a high price: they must always preclude a certain degree of *freedom*. A worm can bend itself anywhere along the length of its body; we can flex our limbs only at those places where joints are located. Every alteration of the supporting structure has, as a prerequisite, the dismantling of certain parts before a reconstruction incorporating the (what are hoped to be) improved adaptations can become possible. Between partial demolition and reconstruction lies, necessarily, a phase of increased vulnerability. (An illustration of this principle is the molting of crustaceans, that portion of a cycle during which an exoskeleton must be cast off so that a larger one may be grown.)

Our species has, I believe, a built-in mechanism whose life-preserving function consists of making alterations of cultural structures possible without, at the same time and during the process, endangering the entire stock of information contained within the tradition of a culture. Similar to the mutation rate that must be correctly gauged in order not to jeopardize the continued evolutionary development of a species, so must the extent of possible changes within every culture be contained and limited. At the approach of puberty, young people begin to loosen their allegiances to group rituals and the norms of social behavior that are being passed on to them by means of family traditions. At the same time they become receptive to new ideals which they can make their own and for which they are prepared to do battle. This molting or shedding of traditional ideas and ideals is a critical phase of human development and brings dangers with it. During this developmental period young people are especially susceptible to indoctrination.

Nonetheless, this dangerous part of human ontogeny is

indispensable since it provides one of the possibilities for effecting alterations in the grand inheritance of the cultural tradition. This crisis involving evaluations of ideals is like an opening door through which new thoughts and ideas and new perceptions and knowledge can gain entry and can become integrated into the structures of a culture. Without this critical process the cultural tradition would remain too rigid. The culture-preserving and, consequently, life-sustaining function of this mechanism has, however, as a necessary precondition, something similar to a state of equilibrium between the immutability of old traditions and the capacity for adaptability through which throwing overboard certain parts of the traditional inheritance cannot be avoided. A preponderance of that which is conservative causes exactly the same result in the biological development of species as in the development of cultures — the formation of "living fossils"; an overabundance of variability, on the other hand, causes in both the formation of abnormalities. As examples of such maldevelopments in social behavior can be cited the emergence of such phenomena as terrorism and the current popularity of quite inept religious sects.

The mechanism being discussed here, whose function it is to facilitate the transmission of the traditional information that has accumulated during the course of cultural development and, at the same time, to open the doors to accommodate the acquisition of new information, has, in our Western culture, obviously gone off the rails, as the abundance of only the just cited abnormalities confirms. A large number of the young people today appear to believe that all of the information contained in our cultural tradition is dispensable because it is not essential. They throw out the *parents* with the bath water; they confront members of the older generation as severe critics. This extreme enmity that now exists between generations has its origin indubitably in the rapidity of the development of our technologically oriented culture. The divisive distance between the interests of one generation and those of the next continues to become greater. As Thomas Mann so marvelously described in his tetralogy, *Joseph and His Brothers,* the cultural remove of one generation from the next in biblical times was so minimal that a son's identification with his father was not only taken as a matter of course but could go so far that a son was able, in fact, to consider himself identical to his father and take his name as his own. With the vastly accelerated increase in the tempo of developments in our civilization, the generations have become more and more unlike one another. An additional fact that cannot be denied is that the amount of tradition which must be thrown overboard by each succeeding generation is increasing steadily. A few decades ago one could, for example, still accept the expression "My country right or wrong" as a proper expression of patriotism; today this standpoint can be regarded as lacking in moral responsibility.

While the generations within each of the industrialized/civilized nations become more and more dissimilar to one another and more alienated, the members of the same generation throughout the world become more and more alike. The extension of worldwide transport facilities and travel possibilities and the ever-expanding communications media permit the earth, as so often is said, to become ever smaller. Characteristics that not so very long ago could still be regarded as national characteristics disappear. Not too many years ago it was still possible to identify with certainty the Germans, the English and the Americans by the cut of their clothes; today this is no longer possible. But most of all the young people of every industrialized country have become similar to one another in external appearances through what they wear and through the way they are groomed.

The emotional bonding to their own symbols and ideals elicited by newly formed groups prevents their members from recognizing how great is the value of the well-tested, passed-on knowledge that they are so readily prepared to dispense with uncompromisingly. It is an error to believe that after the form and content of an old culture are thrown overboard a new and better, ready-made one will quite naturally be brought into being to take its place instantaneously. We must seriously confront the sobering fact that there is no purpose-oriented predeterminism of what happens in our world to protect our culture. We must be clearly aware that we humans, ourselves, bear the burden of responsibility for preserving our culture both from erroneous developments and from rigidity.

The Unplanned Process of Cultural Evolution

Cultures evolve just as all other living systems do — each for itself, each at its own expense and at its own risk and without any preexisting plan. It is very difficult for many people to realize and to accept the fact that the "onward and upward" development of human culture ever "toward the higher" is not at all exclusively guided by a sense of human values, by human insight and by human goodwill.

Even today we do not have a comprehensive overview of all the factors influencing our cultural evolution. It is urgently to be hoped, however, that among the influences a sense of values will come to assume an ever-increasing role. Yet according to the current state of affairs on our planet it would seem that also in the evolution of culture the game engaging everything with everything else is not being played among a multiplicity of specifically set goals but, instead, is being prodded in a direction of universal uniformity commonly agreed to be highly worthwhile by almost everyone alive today. Still it is diversity of the selection pressures, the variety of the challenges, that urges the grand sweep of organic creation upward. Hans Freyer has described how a sudden efflorescence of high cultures can be noted wherever and whenever diverse cultures, for example, agriculturalists and nomadic herders, have come into contact with one another. We must acknowledge the sobering fact that it is not only the ideals and the values of humanity's most exemplary representatives which determine the evolutionary direction of our culture. To a far greater extent this direction appears to be subject to the archaic factors that were already at work affecting the phylogeny of our prehuman ancestors.

It has already been indicated in an earlier passage that creative occurrences become possible apparently only when in the "game engaging everything with everything else" *many* players participate. Such was also the case in the earlier evolution of cultures, as Freyer has depicted it. But today only a single "culture" is setting the standard: all of the highly civilized people on our earth go to war with the same weapons, utilize the same technology and — what is certainly most decisive — trade in the same world market and attempt, using the same means, to compete with one another and to gain some advantage over one another.

In a word: as far as the prospects for a further evolution of our culture are concerned, almost analogous conditions prevail as those in force for the further evolution of an animal species when *intra*specific selection is involved. Because of this the prospects are extraordinarily dismal.

Homo ludens

In a chapter concerned with the processes of creative becoming those that occur within the human brain and — at a collective, social level — those of the human mind must also be discussed. In a unique sense the creative processes that come to pass within the minds of humans, and only in humans, are a game. Friedrich Schiller said that man is only completely human when he plays. If Manfred Eigen and Ruthild Winkler titled their trail-blazing work *Laws of the Game* this signifies, thus, an equating of the creative principle with the interaction and integration of very many single systemic components through whose multifariousness and following the pregiven rules of the game (the "pregiven" part being wondrous and still not completely comprehensible) something is created that we perceive — must so perceive — as a higher entity than the single elements were, in themselves, through which the creation came to be.

Even at the animal level curiosity behavior is very difficult to differentiate from play, and the close relationship between research and play was never more clearly brought home to me than during that felicitous summer when Niko Tinbergen was in Altenberg and we played with the egg-rolling behavior pattern of the graylag goose, about which we then wrote a scientific paper. When Benjamin Franklin drew electrical sparks from the damp kite string, that was certainly no purpose-oriented undertaking having as its goal the invention of the lightning rod.

The strong attracting pull exerted by an established goal inhibits the capacity for "playing around" with the factors through whose combination and recombination a solution to a problem could come. Wolfgang Köhler tells about his chimpanzee, Sultan, and how he abandoned the problem of fetching an unreachable banana with the two lengths of a fishing rod he had available, neither of which was long enough for his purpose when used alone, and how he then played aimlessly with the two sections of rod until he discovered that the pieces could be fitted together. At the very same moment he made this discovery he also recognized that he was now in possession of a tool by means of which he could reach his goal.

Similar processes have probably played a comparable part in every invention of a tool. Later, however, when the now known tool begins to be manufactured, a purely purpose-oriented behavior sets in which we call work. Work can become an end in itself through the "joy of functioning," the joy experienced through exercising one's skills and capabilities, and conjures up its own associated dangers; these will be discussed in chapter 8. But here, in the chapter on creative processes, a different pleasure derived from performing concerns us: the human who has at his command many different kinds of skillful movements is simply incapable of not putting them into action, of not playing with them — and through a combination of such skill and play *art* emerges. The most ancient art form is certainly the dance, the primary elements of which are alluded to in the actions of chimpanzees. But play can also be slipped into the series of actions involved in every purpose-oriented activity, and in the manufacture of some utilitarian object it may be that the worker cannot restrain himself from imparting unnecessary but *beautiful* decorative flourishes to his finished product. The object fabricated by *Homo faber* obtains, through the creative capacity of *Homo ludens,* a remarkable life of its own. In religious realms such fabrications secure for themselves independence by being made over into cult objects, as Hans Freyer has described. Most certainly the earliest of all art objects were of a sacral nature.

Karl Bühler always emphasized that perceiving was an *activity*. Every cognitive capacity is, in the same sense, such an activity, as exploratory behavior is, too. The actively perceived image of the real external world that comes to exist within every organism — be it a ciliate protozoan or a human — is incomplete and various, but provides each organism with the information it needs. These various and incomplete impressions of the surrounding world never contradict one another relative to the real and the external; they differ from one another only through extensiveness and restrictedness of content and detail. However extensive or restricted, this information is always obtained by each organism in that the organism has *done* something to get it.

Exploratory behavior or the behavior motivated by curiosity has developed among humans, phylogenetically as well as ontogenetically, into science. In their intrinsic natures, science and art are as closely related to each other as exploratory behavior is related to play. For their proper functioning, both of them have in common an essential prerequisite: both require, as Gustav Bally has expressed this, using the terminology of Kurt Lewin, a "tensionless field." Expressed in another way: play and exploratory behavior have their own motivations; neither playing nor exploring, as activities, ever appears in the service of another specific motivation. The raven handling an unfamiliar object by treating it, serially, to several of the behavior patterns from its rich repertoire (feeding, fighting, courting, escaping, grooming) is not induced to execute them by the usual "serious situation" motivations associated with the release of each of the action patterns that it exploratively brings into play. Quite the contrary; playful exploration would break off at once if such a "serious" motivation were to rise up in the raven.

In principle all of this is valid for human arts and for human research, just as it applies to the play activities and curiosity behavior of animals. Considered in such a context, there can be, thus, in the strict sense, no "applied art" and still less an "applied science" — there is only an applying of oneself to an art or a science.

The rule *l'art pour l'art* has universal validity. For research very similar rules apply. Freedom as an essence of, and intrinsic to, the game, a prerequisite for every creative coming into being and essential, as well, to phylogenesis, is apparently just as indispensable for the creativity of humans doing research. The way to the goal, or to whatever afterward reveals itself to have been a goal worth striving toward, often leads at the beginning in an entirely unexpected and seemingly roundabout direction. Even a chicken striving toward a coveted piece of bread lying behind a wire lattice has trouble finding the detour around the fence, and the solution to its problem becomes that much more difficult the closer it and the bread are to the fence, and the more intensive the appetitive behavior for the bread becomes. The play of ideas of the researcher dispenses with a narrowly definable goal just as does the game of living forms in phylogenesis. The researcher does not know what he will ultimately find; his Gestalt perception provides him with only approximate information about the direction in which something of interest is "hovering." But what this interesting thing actually is must be transmitted to him through a procedure in which trial and error, hypotheses formulation and attempts to disprove these hypotheses, play roles that appear to resemble the functions carried out by mutation and selection in the game of organic becoming.

Questions exist that humans are permitted to ask even when unanswerability must be presumed, and relative to such questions we are allowed, instead, to speculate: I *believe* that both art and the human striving for cognitive comprehension are manifest forms of the grand game in which nothing more is stipulated than the game's rules; both art and actively solicited perceptions are but special cases of the recurring creative act to which we owe our existence. On this conviction, comparable to a belief, rests, as well, my attempt in the second part of this book to demonstrate the realness, and the life-sustaining importance, of the perceptions by humans of values.

·⟨ PART TWO ⟩·

The Reality of the "Merely" Subjective

What will become of the human race in the future is not foreseeable, but what humanity becomes will be determined by processes at work exclusively within humans themselves. All of the external factors that could contribute to a creative evolution of a genetic or cultural sort have been closed out. Whether all of mankind will become a community of truly humane beings or a strictly controlled organization of disinherited, disfranchised nonhumans depends exclusively upon whether we are capable and ready to allow ourselves to be subjected to guidance by our values, not reasoned but genuinely sensed. If we are to take these values seriously, and if we are to obey them as categorical imperatives, we must first become convinced of their *reality*. To convey this conviction of realness is the task of the second part of my book.

··∘[FOUR]∘··

The Mind-Body Problem

THE LEGITIMATION
OF PHENOMENOLOGICAL EXPERIENCE

In the first part of this book I attempted to refute the erroneous belief that everything happening in the world is predetermined and oriented toward some purpose. I believed this attempt necessary since a firm conviction in a predetermined, definitive purpose for the course of world events relieves humans of individual responsibility and at the same time encourages that passive confidence in progress which, in our time, is having such a pernicious effect.

In the third part of this book I will describe a way of thinking that I designate as "ontological reductionism" and present as synonymous with an epidemic disease of the human mind. The specific sociological and cultural-historical circumstances causing this habit of thought will also be discussed. But beforehand some general epistemological considerations concerning the various cognitive mechanisms of humans are necessary and must anticipate that later discussion now and here.

Simplified, scientism can be defined as the belief that only what can be expressed in the terminology of the exact natural sciences and what can be verified through quantification possess reality. Consequently, measuring and enumerating are the only means of human perception qualifying as valid and scientifically legitimate. But this point of view — that one might possibly formulate a perception "more objectively" by excluding from consideration the apparatus delivering the perception — is false. By comparison, it would be the same as regarding the colored edges which an old, nonachromatic lens allows to appear around all contours to be characteristic of the observed object and not characteristic of the lens of the telescope or microscope being used. The classic example of such an erroneous ascription of characteristics is Goethe's study of color; he regarded color qualities not as products of our perceiving apparatus but as physical properties of light itself. As far as I have been able to determine, the physicist P. W. Bridgman was the first to see the relationship between our human capacities for perceiving and the mechanisms for transmitting our perceptions. He said quite clearly that the process of knowing and the object that is in the process of being known must be studied simultaneously and may not legitimately be separated from each other: the object of knowledge and the instrument of knowledge must be regarded as a unitary whole. My old paradigm of an objectification* process is as follows: I touch the cheek of my grandson and this seems to me to be hot, as if he had a high fever. But I do not for a moment believe

---

*I identify the activity of abstracting constant properties with the verb "objectifying" and its achievement with the noun "objectification."

that the child is sick since I know that I have just come in from the garden, that it is winter, that my hands are very cold and that consequently my tactile perception of degrees of heat has become displaced. Knowledge about this "merely" subjective shift in my perception of heat makes it possible for me to achieve a correct objectification of an external, extrasubjective given.

This taking into account of subjective phenomena along with the laws that apply to them is not only quite generally indispensable for our everyday endeavors to comprehend the external world outside ourselves as objectively as possible, it is also quite particularly indispensable when the human as perceiving subject should be perceived perceiving. For me the term "phenomenology" means this: every attempt at objectification must necessarily include perception of subjective experience and awareness of the laws pertaining to it.

A CRITIQUE OF SCIENTISM AND ITS CRITICS

There are many philosophers who have recognized scientism as an unfortunate encapsulation of the human mind. Regrettably some of them also believe the scientistic view of the world to be a logical and necessary consequence of research in the natural sciences and such research, thus, to be a bane for humanity. Lord Snow writes about art, meaning the humanities, and science, meaning the natural sciences, as forming two cultures which, having separated, can never be brought together again. The Viennese physicist Herbert Pietschmann speaks in his book *Das Ende des naturwissenschaftlichen Zeitalters* [The end of the natural science era] about "two streets," one of which leads to the perception of what is correct while the other leads to the perception of what is true. He goes on to say: "Correct is what can be verified, in extreme cases by means of mathematics, but just at that juncture the relationship to reality is lost. True, in contrast, is only a concretely experienced situation which, because it is unique, must for this reason remain forever unverifiable." Pietschmann goes so far as to limit the systemic scope of all natural scientific perception to the aggregate of all those facts that are in stock and available "intersubjectively," that is, facts that, each on the basis of its qualitative characteristics, can be proved by every single person to be logically irrefutable.

In the book *Unbegreifliches Geheimnis* [Incomprehensible secret], Erwin Chargaff states: "The great philosophers of the pre-Socratic period — perhaps the profoundest thinkers the West has ever known — were so pervaded by the immeasurableness of the surrounding world that every measurement would have seemed to them a mismeasurement, every weighing as too daring." Using sharp words, Chargaff says that research done in the natural sciences progresses, of necessity, toward "smaller and smaller measurable minutiae" and that an overview encompassing the whole is lost.

Chargaff's criticism of natural science research expressly excludes the observations undertaken and carried out in the study of animal behavior: "I am not talking here about a Tinbergen or a von Frisch," he says, "since, for me, their work exemplifies the most honest natural science done in the old manner of watching and noting and arriving at judgments. But it would have to be a most unusual molecular biologist who could still acknowledge this kind of research as being biology." This charge made against molecular biologists is not justified. They would not be molecular biologists if they were not interested in biology, and I know quite a few of them personally who are also well acquainted with the work being done in such specialized areas as comparative animal behavior.

The critics of analytical natural science are to be reproached for also believing, apparently, that only what is measurable is real or, at least, everything not quantifiable is incomprehensible and, in principle, not knowable. They seem also to imply that we humans have access to such things as those that are unquantifiable only by means of revelatory experience. At the same time — and this is a further error — they apparently equate the unknowable with the supernatural or with the extranatural. Usually they also seem to sense, perhaps without deliberate reflection, that every causal explanation is somehow a profanation of what is being explained.

One knows that the right and left halves of the human brain accomplish equally important cognitive functions. One knows that in the left hemisphere the capacities for logical thinking and for speech are localized, and that the right hemisphere sustains most of our emotional experiences as well as (and above all) the synoptic, comprehensive integration of all experience — expressed without qualms, our Gestalt perception.

Whoever is convinced of the correctness and truth of the theory of evolution (here I use intentionally both of Pietschmann's terms and the meanings he has given them) can identify neither with the epistemological position of scientism nor with that of scientism's critics. He is convinced that for research in the natural sciences he needs to use Gestalt perception, but he also knows that with this perception he is actually only at the beginning of the scientific work, in that what must follow is the task of producing proof of the Gestalt perception's correctness — here, again, in Herbert Pietschmann's sense of the term.

Whoever is convinced that what I have called the *Weltbildapparat* [world-imaging apparatus] — the physiological mechanism providing humans with conceptual images of their external world, what Karl Popper has called the "perceiving apparatus" — has come into being during aeons of evolutionary development and by means of adaptation to circumstances extant in a real external world and, in the process of coming to be what it is, has accumulated and stored massive amounts of information which allow humans to formulate conceptualized images of external reality that are, in fact, more or less adequate for human purposes, can be misled by the two positions discussed above and presented as reciprocating errors. In his time Charles Darwin expressed my thesis more concisely and very clearly: what is astonishing is not how many things are left unremarked by perception, but how many highly complicated things far removed from our practical lives are nevertheless permitted by our sensory system to form an image.

For the evolutionary epistemologist the problem posed by the cleft between the two cultures defined by Lord Snow and the two diverging streets described by Herbert Pietschmann is a pseudoproblem that arises primarily because, although Snow and Pietschmann are opponents of scientistic reductionism, they overestimate the efficacy of logic and mathematics. If one does not regard these functions of perception as the only legitimate ones, and if one does grant the nonratiocinative capacities of our perceiving apparatus, including Gestalt perception, the significance they deserve, one is no longer surprised by the contradictions arising among the various results of our manifold cognitive capabilities. Werner Heisenberg has said that the laws of mathematics are not the laws of nature but rather those of a very distinct mechanism of human nature.

The apparent irreconcilability of the perceptions transmitted independently of one another by means of the various cognitive functions, especially the incompatibility of

logical thinking and Gestalt perception, is further emphasized by the typological differences of the researchers involved. The analytic thinkers criticized by Chargaff and
Pietschmann are obviously more often less gifted for "seeing"
the interconnections within more complexly integrated systems. For Goethe, that great seer, it was just the opposite.
He scorned analytic thinking and its results. Evidently those
people with logical-analytical talents, and those whose talents for Gestalt perception respond to larger systems, turn
with fair regularity to different branches of scientific research, which only makes communication between them
that much more problematic. Whoever has accepted that
the perceiving apparatus of humans is a system that has come
into being during the course of evolution does not feel it
to be a contradiction of the principles of natural science, as
Erwin Chargaff does, that we are surrounded by "incomprehensible secrets." For the evolutionist "incomprehensible" is not supernatural or extranatural. There are, in fact,
"a sheer unending number of things that are entirely natural
and yet, for our brain, completely incomprehensible" — as
Carl Zuckmayer lets his rat catcher say so beautifully. That
primitive, in principle unpredictable, mass of simplified
impressions that our perceiving apparatus transmits to us
from the real external world can be compared, let us say,
to the knowledge an Eskimo has about the biology of the
seal or of the whale, animals on which his life depends. Most
prominent in his picture of these animals will be those characteristics of the prey that for him, as a hunter, are the most
important to know. If we attempt to visualize the way of
life of our ancestors at the time they were becoming human
and the various sorts of selection pressures that influenced
the evolution of their perceiving apparatus then, there is no
need for us to wonder why very many things, even today,

still remain imperceptible. Much more amazing to us should be the realization that our archaic world-perceiving apparatus is capable of reproducing images of things that, for our ancestors only a few centuries ago, had absolutely no significance whatsoever. We are also astonished by the universal application of our forms of conceptualization and of our eidetic images that facilitate the shaping, in our minds, of a model of the surrounding spatial structure, that so-called space model of the central nervous system, and by the abstracting capacity of our Gestalt perception whose functions make it possible for our conceptual thinking to transcend the prior boundaries of the imaginable — of earlier conceptual categories and of former eidetic images — in order to be able to contemplate the unimaginable.

When one has grasped these actually banal axiomatic aspects of the evolutionary theory of knowledge, one is no longer amazed that our world-perceiving apparatus has sometimes developed *two* differentiated receiving mechanisms for the imaging of a *single* extrasubjective given. This does not plunge us into logical difficulties when we realize that something which is, in itself, one and the same can appear to us to be something quite different depending on our access to it, how we approach it. For example, an electron can sometimes be perceived as a particle, at other times as a wave, and it can — to illustrate the extreme inconstancy of perception — be in two places at the same time. Our compelling need for logic screams to high heaven; nevertheless, we must accustom ourselves to this state of affairs. The genetically programmed receiving mechanisms that transmit information to us about extrasubjective reality are comparable to windows providing us views in various directions or allowing us to see two "sides" of one and the same reality that are totally different and stand in no apparent logical relationship to one another. Physiological and psychical processes are, in this a-logical way (as Max Hartmann says), identical to one another. Matter and energy are also identical in this way, and the same is true for space and time.

Since we know that the entire physiological-psychical organization of our thinking, just as all other organic structures, came into being during the course of phylogeny, we are not about to grant its reports absolute validity. Nevertheless, our confidence in them is strengthened by the fact that two means of perception-cognition, physiologically different from one another, reach the same conclusions; these conclusions are results brought to completion by the abstracting capacities of Gestalt perception, on the one hand, and of logical-rational reasoning on the other. The functional similarities between the two are so close that the discoverer of these processes, Herman Helmholtz, regarded these accomplishments of perception-cognition as unconscious reasoning. In point of fact the complex reckoning processes of perception-cognition are physiological processes that are not accessible to our self-observation. Among these reckoning processes are the so-called constancy phenomena; that of color constancy can be cited as an example. The "computer" involved calculates the constantly inherent color of a thing using two characteristic reflection factors: the color of the lighting prevalent at the moment and the wavelength reflecting at the moment from the thing being observed. The result is reported immediately as the sensed "color of the object." One knows that this process is not organized and regulated by deliberate rational objectification; Karl von Frisch has shown that the honeybee has the same color-constancy mechanism available for its use as does the human. When, in an experiment, one falsifies the "premises" of these calculating processes, one gets the corresponding predictable erroneous perceptions. As Erich von Holst has proved, most of what are known as optical illusions are based on this very same principle. Egon Brunswik called these capacities of perception-cognition *ratiomorphous* in order to convey their analogousness to rational processes but, as well, their psychophysiological disparateness.*

The analogy of rational thought processes — which even the most radical believers in and practitioners of scientism recognize as scientifically legitimate — with the ratiomorphous capacities of perception is a very pressing argument for the contention that these cognitive capacities, although certainly not of a rational nature, must still be recognized as being, as well, legitimate sources of scientific knowledge. Rational processes and ratiomorphic processes combine to form yet another example of the proclivity that our perceiving apparatus often evinces for training and qualifying two different, independently functioning organs for mastering the same task.

Neglecting a cognitive capacity signifies denying access to available knowledge. This is the greatest offense a human can commit against the intellectual ideal of searching for truth. The means used and the ways taken by behaviorists as they proceed, renouncing and forgoing as a source of knowledge that aspect of behavior associated with experience, can be compared to the actions of a person who, for reasons not possible to determine, continuously keeps one eye closed and thereby robs himself of stereoscopic vision. The simile limps because the loss of information through

---

*"Ratiomorphous" includes all those sensory and nerve processes that take place in areas of our central nervous system that are completely inaccessible to our consciousness and self-observation. Although clearly analogous to rational behavior in both formal and functional respects, they have nothing to do with conscious reasoning. See *Behind the Mirror,* p. 119.

monocular vision is, by comparison, much less, but it provides a transition to yet another example: some critics of
ontological reductionism keep both eyes open but, where
the real world is actually a unity, they see double. Lord
Snow sees two nonunifiable cultures; Herbert Pietschmann
sees two streets, one of which leads to the true and the
beautiful while the other leads to the scientifically correct.

THE INDUBITABILITY OF EXPERIENCE

Our *subjective* experience is, to an extent that seems remarkable, underestimated by many scientists. Even its definition provided by some reference works is denigrating:
"biased," "prejudiced" and "subject to contingent valua-
tions" are among the descriptive words and phrases used.
Even those philosophers who do command complete insight
into the epistemological consequences of ontological reductionism or scientism see in the study of subjective experience, in phenomenology, no source of scientific
knowledge. Herbert Pietschmann states in *Das Ende des naturwissenschaftlichen Zeitalters* that the aspiration of the sciences to arrive at an "intersubjective" conceptualized image
of the world deflects our pursuit of knowledge away from
humans themselves and withdraws more and more from
man's specific problems. When we "attempt to enter the
realm of the individual," Pietschmann says, we move into
the "private sphere," into the "less real part of reality," which
is "merely subjective" and, for that reason, not interesting.
In another passage Pietschmann says: "Natural science concerns itself only with intersubjective phenomena and delib-
erately disregards the human individual."

Pietschmann's statement is undoubtedly intended as a
reproach of the scientistic way of thinking; thus what he
says leaves ethologists and evolutionary epistemologists un-

offended since they do, in fact, understand that natural science is something quite different. Natural science not only can but must take simply everything that exists in the world as a subject for its research. And, as I have explained in an earlier section, the objectivity that is necessary for such research can be approached only through simultaneous observations of both the human apparatus that perceives images of the external world and the external objects that form the images being perceived. The process of knowing and the objects being known cannot legitimately be disassociated from each other.

Even allowing for these epistemological considerations, it is simply not so that subjective experience is the exclusive concern of some private sphere of the lone human individual. We can be thankful that in emotions, and especially in the realm of perceived values, there is shared commonality — in the emotions released within every normal human through particular external circumstances, such as, for example, the indignation we feel when the rights of fellow humans are seriously violated. Innate programs certainly play a role in such situations; yet there are also culturally conditioned sensibilities that have quite general dissemination. Wilhelm Furtwängler reports that when a new musical work is first performed, virtually no relationship exists between its value as a composition and the success it has with the listening public. Symphonies and operas that today are universally treasured were failures at their premieres. With time, however, the true worth of a musical work of art makes itself felt in a justifiable way, says Furtwängler; in the course of his career he ascertained that a majority of his audience placed approximately the same relative value on various operas that he did himself.

Based on genetic programming are not only the apparatuses for sensory perception and for logical thinking that outline and fill in with color the picture we have of our world; also based on these programs are the complicated feelings that determine our interhuman behavior. Our social behavior especially is dominated by an immensely old heritage of species-specific action and reaction patterns; these are undoubtedly much, much older than the specific capacities of intelligence associated with our neocortex, that is, with the evolutionarily youngest part of our brain. The rational capabilities of the neocortex serve, to a much greater extent, the interactions humans have with their *extra*specific environment; for these interactions with the external environment the older species-specific action and reaction patterns concerned primarily with interhuman behavior can be neglected without causing very much harm. Ontological reductionism and scientistic circumscriptions of knowledge do not have such a deleterious effect on extraspecific interactions as they do where interpersonal behavior is concerned. Human reason {*Vernunft*} and human intellect [*Verstand*] often only appear to exert authority over human emotions. About these latter we simply *know* too little to be able to channel them competently, and the little that is currently known appears to be made use of by hardly anyone except the experts at advertising agencies and by demagogues.

In scientistically oriented natural science it is virtually forbidden to speak about qualities of feeling because these are neither definable in the language of the exact natural sciences nor are they expressible in exactly measured quantities. The more decisively one defines human perception and cognition as that which is capable of being expressed in words, that much clearer it becomes how many essentially fundamental phenomena cannot be expressed directly in words. Ludwig Wittgenstein, who, in his logic, was close to positivism (the theory that positive knowledge is based on natural phenomena and that their properties and relations are verifiable by the empirical sciences), said that he "wanted to set limits to thinking [*dem Denken*] or, much more, not to thinking but to the expression of thoughts [*dem Ausdruck der Gedanken*]." The interpretation made by K. Wuchterl and A. Hübner, that "everything *spoken* about the meaning of life, about ultimate truth, about the good and the beautiful, about God, can only miss the mark since, although [conceptualizations of] all these are in fact existent, they are inexpressible," is quite right.

Qualities of experience can assuredly not be defined in terms of language, as I will later show in connection with the simple quality "red." Despite this (according to Max Hartmann) a-logical relationship between physiological and subjective processes, the correlation between both of them is so reliable that a subjective phenomenon, for example, the perception of a complementary color, can be utilized, through known contrast phenomenon, as a dependable indicator of the parallel process that is being carried out physiologically, for which Erich von Holst's work on deception of the senses has provided the proof. The argument that everything realized as experience exclusively through looking inward, through self-observation, is "merely subjective," that is, possesses no objective reality, carries no consequential weight. When reading the results provided by a measuring instrument, we also obtain knowledge through subjective experience in that what is experienced is the perception of a moving red indicator that has, as a background, a graduated scale in black and white. The basis of all our experience of the external world is formed by our primary knowledge, the data of initial experience. Wolfgang Metzger called this knowledge the "fore-found" or "pre-discovered." Donald Campbell called it "proximal knowledge" in contradistinction to "distal knowledge," that which we acquire indirectly after making combinations and deductive evaluations of primary experience, after "checking whether it fits."

Our emotions, above all the feelings we have for values, belong without exception to that extensive sector of real processes which are "in fact existent," yet "inexpressible." In their subjective quality they are almost impossible to define with words, but through experimental research they can be made tangible — through investigations of those external stimulus situations in which they are elicited and occur. It is beyond doubt that a great number of qualitative emotions, recognizable and unmistakable, are common to all mankind, that is, are anchored in the genes of humans.

ART AS A SOURCE OF PHENOMENOLOGICAL KNOWLEDGE

Although, as I have said, the qualities of experience are not subject to definition, the unsayable is still capable of being expressed: artists can do this. The composer whose work speaks directly to the heart does not even need the spoken word. But even in words the unsayable allows itself to be said, as the art of poetry teaches us.

Simply from the universal comprehensibility of literature it follows that the art of poetry has, as subject, quite generally all that is commonly human and quite particularly the emotions of mankind. When we read the *Epic of Gilgamesh,* the *Odyssey,* Shakespeare's dramas or a novel, we are always able to empathize with the experiences presented as part of the portrayal of the protagonists. They experience love and hate, friendship, jealousy, envy, desire and sorrow, fear and anger exactly as we do.

An author can describe experience only as simile or as metaphor. What he makes graphic and what he does, above all, to elicit empathy is to describe a human situation in which the ascribed emotions would naturally appear and conform with the lawfulnesses of human nature. Such stimulus situations, quite objectively delineable, tally with the released emotions. Artists and authors are constrained in their presentations to these relatively limited number of situations; for any others the listener or reader has, quite literally, no "organ," no receptor mechanism, for deciphering the message. We can justifiably assume that the foundation of our emotions is formed by universally human inborn behavior programs, primarily innate releasing mechanisms.

Because of this we should not be amazed when, in the literature of the world — all the way from (again) the *Epic of Gilgamesh* through to the most recently published novels — the same salient thematic elements are used and recur again and again: the hero who frees the maiden held captive; the friend who despite all dangers stands by his friend; social themes such as the strong oppressing the weak, the rich exploiting the poor; the abandoned and helpless child. Nor does just the poet or author, because of commitment and conviction, make use of these motifs. Even the purely mercantile producers of novels, plays and films know how to appeal to their audiences through the innate releasing mechanisms mentioned. Yes, in some cases they can do this much better because they know how coolly to calculate average human reactions, reactions they have probed and fathomed through successes achieved and failures noted in the methods of commercial advertising.

They use their models with less feeling for their subjects than Tinbergen shows for his sticklebacks. The creative human expresses his emotions and does not think about possible public reception; the commercial producer collects what he knows from public reaction. The poet himself experiences specific human emotions; the producer of art lets his public experience them. Both Mörus in Schiller's *Bürgschaft* [Standing surety] and the hero in any western defend the friend in danger with the same self-sacrifice.

Products put together following commercial prescriptions provide, in a certain sense, especially good starting points for researching our emotions. These products show us how much the model of a releasing object can be simplified and these simplifications exaggerated without sacrificing any of the object's effect as a releaser. I know many serious and critical people who know very well what, for them, is "kitsch" and what is "art" and are still incapable of evading the effect of the most primitive kitsch.

THREE HYPOTHESES CONCERNING THE MIND-BODY PROBLEM

No one doubts that close connections exist between certain processes occurring within our bodies and the form in which we experience them. We see the red rose unequivocally in its color and can recognize the rose again by means of it. We know a lot about the circumstances under which the experience of seeing the color red *regularly* and predictably takes place — not only when light of a particular wavelength meets our eye, but also as a so-called contrast effect when the complementary color green is beamed at a significant part of the retina. When this is done we perceive, on the remaining part of the retina not subjected to the beam and even when no red light meets the eye, the color red. One can readily use such a qualitative experience as an *indicator* of a quite specific physiological process, something that sensory physiologists have been doing for a very long time.

The phenomenon of simultaneous contrast described above is a side effect of the processes that compute the reflectional qualities of an object by calculating the color of the illumination (daylight at dawn, lamplight from a hundred-watt bulb with coated glass) together with the wavelength being reflected by the object at the moment — a typical "unconscious conclusion," a reckoning whose realization has nothing to do with the reasoned processes of induction or deduction. Thus the isomorphism between what happens physiologically and what happens subjectively can be quite extensive and very reliable.

To explain this isomorphism there are three valid hypotheses that, epistemologically, are equally legitimate. From the standpoint of the evolutionary theory of knowledge, however, only one of these hypotheses is possible. The first of the three is that of *interaction.* One can take what happens physiologically as the cause of the corresponding experience and assume that this, in turn, has a retroactive effect on the physiological occurrence. This initially quite comprehensible and plausible, roughly causal interrelationship deceives; along with the assumption goes a so-called *metabasis eis allo genos:* a logically inadmissible skipping back and forth between *two* parallel chains of ensuing events that are logically independent of each other. When, for example, someone is slapped solidly in the face by someone else, the experience can be described in the following way: the slapped person senses shock and feels pain; for the moment he is deeply dejected and his self-confidence is reduced substantially. But within seconds his depression gives way to wrath, his self-confidence ragingly demands restitution and finds this in the pleasurable return of the said slap.

A physiologist who pays no attention to experiential processes would describe the same series of events in the following way: a severe jolting of the head and the atlas vertebra along with a simultaneously vigorous stimulation of certain sensory nerve ends produces, in the sympathetic nervous system, an abrupt decrease in the tone and contractibility of smooth muscle; this effect spreads to the central nervous system and a temporary paralysis of the voluntary muscu-lature follows. The person who has been slapped stands there for a moment not only as if paralyzed, he is actually partially paralyzed. He lets his head hang down and turns pale since, when the sympathetic nervous system shuts down, the blood sinks into the abdominal cavity. Immediately af-terward, in a well-known physiological contrast effect, the paralyzed sympathetic nervous system springs back to its opposite state, vehement agitation; the blood flows back up into the head, the sunken eyes bulge out and, instead of sagging muscles, motor excitation sets in. Finally, the in-stinctive movements of combat, such as striking and biting, are released. The drive-satisfying proprioceptive and extero-ceptive reafference of the returned slap leads to satisfaction and to the disappearance of the excitation.

Now it is quite correct, from the physical side as well as from the psychical side, to see in the slap that the recipient unexpectedly sustained the cause of the entire chain of events. But it is incorrect to say that a person is dejected because the equilibrium between sympathetic nerve excitation and vagus nerve excitation has been shifted toward a predomi-nance of the latter and that for this reason a person lets his head hang down. Letting the head hang down has become quite generally recognized as a symbolic indication of sor-row *because* it is the expression of a very specific internal nervous situation that, with reliable regularity, is accom-panied by the subjective indications of depression. *The one cannot be the cause of the other since, in a certain sense, the one is itself the other, except that it is experienced from the other side.*

The second theory (or hypothesis), the doctrine of *psycho-physical parallelism,* maintains that two such chains of events do just that — proceed parallel to one another but, basically, stand in no logical relationship to one another. To date, even the most intensively thorough inquiry into physiological processes, especially those physiological processes of the nerves and of the brain, is still incapable of bringing us one jot nearer to an appreciation of the mind-body problem. Even if we were able, as we are on the physiological side, to comprehend precisely (and to the ideal extent of complete and consistent predictability) many of the processes accessible to investigation on the experiential side, we would still be justified in saying only what Gustav Kramer has already said so sarcastically, that psychophysical parallelism is, indeed, extremely parallel.

No one contests that all experiential processes are accompanied by neural-physiological occurrences, but this sentence cannot be turned around and remain true. There are highly complicated physiological processes going on within the central nervous system that are equivalent to the most complicated calculating operations known, yet these are carried out completely unconsciously.

On the other hand, self-observation reveals to us that very often we have unquestionable, and qualitatively unmistakable, subjective experiences that, as far as we currently know, are not correlated with objective and measurable physiological occurrences. That even the most fleeting thought, the faintest welling of a feeling, has corresponding physiological equivalents cannot be proved. Still, all of us know transitions from such "merely mental" processes to those for which a physiological correlate can unambiguously be demonstrated and proved. The juxtaposition as expressed in the terminology of psychophysical parallelism thus falters twice over: there are nervous-physiological processes without determinable psychical correlates, and there are opposite, subjective processes whose physiological correspondence is not provable. Our assumption that this correlate is, nevertheless, very definitely there, has good reasons. Together with this assumption we anticipate the possibility that these physiological processes are of such delicacy and minimal energy that they will never be traceable.

The third possible approach to the mind-body problem, and the only one that is tenable for the evolutionary epistemologist, is based on the assumption that body and mind, physiological and emotional occurrences, are, in reality, in themselves, simply *one and the same,* and that we experience and recognize them — as we do matter and energy, or energy radiated in the form of waves or particles — by means of two independent and incommensurable cognitive capacities.

The razor-edge demarcation visualized as existing between objective-physiological processes and those of the experiential is there, remarkably, only for our intellects, for our attempts at understanding, and not for our emotions, not for what we sense and not for what we feel. As far as I know, Karl Bühler was the first to recognize clearly that, for every normal person, accepting the existence of fellow humans who have natures very much like one's own and similar sensibilities was something just as obvious as accepting a mathematical axiom. Even idealistic philosophers such as Kant and Schopenhauer were never in doubt about the existence of like-natured fellow humans — although they certainly did not accept evidence of the senses as providing images of external reality, and even though they could have had their knowledge about the existence of similarly sensible fellow creatures only through, alas, the much-disdained evidence provided by those organs of sensory perception.

I contend now: when I say, "There sits my friend Hans," I certainly mean by what I say not just his physiologically explorable corporeality nor just his subjective experientiality (which I am prevented from questioning because of *Du-evidence**), but I do, instead, most certainly mean the *unity of both,* the whole that is both, the entirety that is Hans. I further maintain that what I mean is not only true for me but is true for everyone. Of the three hypothetical positions or approaches to the mind-body problem discussed in this section, the only one that is consistent and without contradiction is the assumption that body and mind are *identical.*

---

*The expression was coined by Karl Bühler. *Du* = you, the familiar form, as against the formal form (*Sie*), of address used by very good and old friends, among relatives, and among members of particular social classes and professional groups. Implied is extensive and mutual personal knowledge (actually acquired or merely presumed) over time and/or through shared aspects of identification, shared ideas and experiences. Also implied is intimate, accepting knowledge of another person's very own unmistakable individuality and a subsequent feeling of commonality this knowledge engenders.

·⦂⟦ FIVE ⟧⦂·

The Phenomenology of Perceived Values

TELEONOMIC VALUATION NORMS

William McDougall's assumption, just as appropriate as it was audacious, that humans have as many instincts as they have qualitatively differentiable emotions, is certainly correct to the extent that a majority of our qualitatively determinable emotions are based on neural and sensorial systems whose structure has evolved phylogenetically and has become genetically fixed. According to Paul Weiss's definition, "A system is anything unitary enough to deserve a name." This definition expresses a high but justified degree of confidence in the subtlety of feeling for psychological connotations that a naturally evolved language possesses. The number of qualitatively unmistakable emotions, such as hate, love, jealousy, envy, friendship, sorrow, mother love, enthusiasm, indignation, joy, is, as has been said, narrowly limited.

These experienced qualities are just as generally human

as *Du-evidence* or a prioristic forms of experience. The several separate innate potentialities for realizing the various emotions *are,* in fact, inborn forms of experience. They correspond to the phylogenetically programmed behavior norms of humans that, within various cultures, have been overlaid by tradition in somewhat different ways; still, the assertion is allowed that they belong, with the highest probability, to a species-preserving, meaningful system of human social life and are, thus, in Pittendrigh's sense, teleonomic.

EXCESS AND DEFICIENCY

The assumption that the emotionally directed behavior norms cited above can be teleonomic appears, at first, to be contradicted by the fact that some of them are valued as positive whereas others are assessed as negative. Enthusiasm and fidelity to friends are deemed praiseworthy; hate and envy are condemned; mother love is regarded as something noble; the nagging fear of never getting one's proper share is thought to be despicable — although both of the last two expressions of human behavior are reckoned among the instinctive aspects of man's "ethogram," the inventory of phylogenetically programmed behavior patterns proper to the species. I believe this apparent contradiction can be explained in the following way: we humans possess a fine sense for determining whether, in the society in which we live, a deficiency of a specific behavior pattern prevails or if it is being proffered in excess. Both, excesses as well as deficiencies, produce disturbances in the equilibrium of a superordinated system.

To illustrate what I mean, I will take something comparable from the history of medicine. Among physicians, comprehension of and appreciation for the states of equilibrium that must prevail within a living system came about, for the most part, scientifically and historically, through studies made of the endocrine-gland system and its disturbances. The Swiss surgeon Kocher was the first to attempt a cure of Basedow's disease, caused by an excessive secretion of thyroid-gland hormones, by removing the thyroid gland. The patients he operated on subsequently died after showing symptoms of what Kocher termed *cachexia thyropriva,* symptoms that were related to those associated with myxedema and that arise through a lack of iodine. From this Kocher correctly concluded that Basedow's disease as well as myxedema were caused by the amount of the endocrine-secreted hormone released, that is, from excessive or deficient thyroxine formation. This was a first step toward a recognition that, among healthy people, there existed among the functions of the endocrine glands a complicated and well-balanced equilibrium of antagonistic effects. Because the complications of these antagonisms are still not thoroughly understood, any arbitrary manipulation of the hormonal system is, even today, irresponsible.

Ronald Hargreaves, a psychiatrist who died much too early, wrote me in one of his last letters that, when confronted by an unknown disturbance, he made it a duty always to ask two questions simultaneously: "What is the original teleonomic function of the system here disturbed?" and "Is the disturbance perhaps determined only by an excessive or a deficient function?" There are many cases for which posing Hargreaves's double question can be meaningful. In the sensory and nervous system of humans, and among the numerous but nonetheless numerable motivations it forms, there apparently exists a balanced interaction analogous to the one sustaining the equilibrium within the system of the endocrine glands.

No reasonable person can doubt that our Western civilization is a system that has been thrown out of equilibrium. No one who thinks scientifically can doubt that all of us together can achieve a restoration of this equilibrium only on the basis of causal insight into both the interplay of the normal functions and what is disturbing the state of balance. Such insight into the system of human social behavior no doubt requires, as a prerequisite, a medical perspective. As the example of the endocrine functions demonstrated, identifying the pathological disturbance is very often helpful for comprehending causal interrelationships.

If, as I have assumed, we humans have a fine sense for determining which forms of behavior in our culture are in short supply and which are rampant, disturbing the state of equilibrium, then, in this "sense," a pronounced teleonomic form of reaction can also be assumed. Here it makes no difference whether the behavior norms involved are cultural, that is, bound to tradition, or genetically programmed. It is entirely possible that the sense for determining deficiency and excess of behavior patterns has been bred into us humans during the course of our evolution. This supposition of possibility also pertains to value perceptions of the beautiful and the ugly, of good and of evil, that will be discussed now.

PERCEPTIONS OF BEAUTY AND DOMESTICATION

A puzzling relationship exists between our sense of the beautiful and the manifestations of domestication (already described in the first part of this book) that appear in virtually all domestic animals and also in civilized humans. When compared to wild forms, in a great majority of all domestic animals — be these birds or mammals — the long, hollow cylindrical bones as well as the base of the skull have become shortened, the connective tissue has loosened, and the tone of the striated musculature has been reduced. There exists, as well, a pronounced proclivity for the accumulation of fat. If one presents pictures of various domestic animals together with those of their undomesticated ancestral forms, as I have done in my lectures and as I have already described earlier in this book, virtually everyone finds the wild form "noble" and beautiful, and in contrast, the domestic form markedly ugly. As I mentioned earlier, Julian Huxley speaks about a "vulgarization" of the domestic animal.

Which human preferences predominated in the selection for ugliness in domestic animals can be postulated with tolerable certainty. Among animals intended to serve humans as food, it is understandable that realizing enjoyment in movement and in the strength of their bodies and in all the behavior patterns that played a role in association with such enjoyment would not be desired and, on the other hand, that the tendency to put on fat would. Where other kinds of selection pressures were being exerted, as, for example, on some breeds of horses and on carrier pigeons, domestic forms remain just as "noble" as the wild forms and, in fact, can even exceed wild forms in those distinctive features usually endangered by the consequences of domestication.

It is possible to imagine that these value estimates placed on the characteristics found in wild forms have a human innate releasing mechanism as their base. Speaking as witnesses for this speculation are all the representations made of the human body in which characteristics of the "wild" form can be exaggerated beyond all moderate measure. Artists of the most varied cultural epochs — Babylonian, Assyrian and Greek painters and sculptors — have emphasized precisely those attributes of the human body, especially those of the human male body, that are threatened by domestication: broad shoulders, narrow hips, long extremities and strong musculature. Can one here, too, perhaps from the realized possibility of producing overemphasized single characteristics, conclude the presence of an innate releasing mechanism (IRM)? This comes more clearly to the fore in representations subject to commercial or ideological influences than in works of art created for their own sake. In the former, and judging from the emphasis, the distorted proportions of the portrayed characteristics are probably wild-form features endangered by domestication. It is hardly necessary to describe in detail how the characteristic proportions of the female figure can also be exaggerated immoderately — the length of the legs, the slimness of the waist, the fullness of the bosom. That it is possible, through exaggeration of characteristics, to produce models having supernormal effectiveness has been authenticated experimentally among animals by N. Tinbergen and G. Baerends. Once when Baerends, during a lecture, showed a film in which an oystercatcher could be seen attempting to brood on an overlarge egg spotted bright blue and black while its own clutch of eggs lay abandoned nearby, an American journalist who happened to be present expressed quite correctly the point of view being advocated here when he exclaimed: "Why, that's the cover girl!"

EVALUATIONS OF DOMESTICATION MANIFESTATIONS IN BEHAVIOR

In a way similar to the negative rating our feeling for values, without deliberate consideration, assigns to the physical manifestations of domestication, we also feel that certain modifications of behavior regularly found among the most diverse domestic animals — and certainly among civilized humans as well — are uncomely and "vulgar." Most domestic animals are less selective than their wild ancestral forms about what they eat and, accordingly, they eat more. Much the same applies to the sexual behavior of many domesticated animals, mammals as well as birds. The negative valuation expressed by the word "bestial" and the meaning given to that word result from the circumstance that humans are best acquainted with domestic animals.

Studies completed by Werner Schmidt, and my studies done much earlier, which concentrated on a comparison between the graylag goose and the house goose descended from it, brought out especially striking examples of vulgarization in sexual behavior. The sexual behavior of purebred female graylag geese is subject to strong inhibitions that can be overcome only through long personal acquaintance with a gander and, above all, through a very complicated ritual. The courtship conducted by the gander and the hesitant acquiescence of the goose are, in so many aspects, analogous to human pair formation that through an exact presentation of them one attracts the scorn of all those who know nothing about analogies. Among house geese, and even among the hybrids resulting from crossings of house geese with wild forms, most of these inhibitions have disappeared; the human observer cannot avoid perceiving the frankly open sexual overtures a house goose makes to a partner she hardly knows as something vulgar, something decadent. We also react to our fellow humans in a similar way. The modifications of behavior typical for domestication are not perceived as evil but as vulgar. They do not provoke dread or horror, as murder does or another violent crime would do, but, instead, a feeling of another quality, one closer to contempt and abhorrence and disgust.

If one assumes that the highly specialized rituals of pair formation possess teleonomic value, a value that is difficult to doubt, then it also lies within the realm of the possible that we humans also possess programmed reactions which serve to protect and preserve proven ritualized forms of social behavior. Rituals of this sort constitute, as it were, the skeleton of the social structure and, for the present discourse, it is immaterial if the base of these stable structures is imbedded in the genome or only in the tradition of a culture. Collected protocols accumulated to date for graylag geese permit the statement that the procreative success of individual geese, measured on the basis of raised goslings that leave their parents during the spring following their birth, stands in direct relationship to the durability of pair bonding. To this can be added that, among vertebrates which form pairs and where both sexes are involved in rearing the young, the rituals of courtship put on display those characteristics that also have important functions for brood care and, above all, for defense of the progeny. The gander demonstrates aggressiveness and courage in the face of stronger opponents as well as vigilance. The often cited "triumph ceremony" is both an outward, ritualized demonstration of readiness to attack and an inward demonstration of the greatest tenderness toward the family. Comparable behavior can be found as early in evolutionary time as that suggested by bony fishes which also live together in bonded pairs. The teleonomy of all these courtship formalities that anticipate later behaviors associated with brood tending lies, apparently, in the opportunity the female is provided to choose from among those vying for her attention the one who is prospectively the best family father. The gander can also be seen attracting attention to his strength by taking off into the air unnecessarily often, by quickly accelerating to exaggeratedly high speeds and by braking just as sharply. Both of the latter actions are also performed by young stallions and by young male humans in a similar manner — by the human sometimes on or in a motorized vehicle.

The teleonomic fulfillment of these behavior patterns has, as a prerequisite, that the female possess a finely tuned sense for the quality of those who are courting her, but also, together with this, that the pair formations that culminate in this way be monogamous, at least on the part of the female. The careful choosing of the partner in accordance with teleonomic qualities relevant to the sociologically familial would not make much sense if, subsequently, the female were to be fertilized by just any male. That only female graylag geese are absolutely monogamous also favors the interpretation of monogamous pair formation made here. Among ganders the behavior sequences leading to copulation can be released even when disassociated from the behaviors of pair formation; among females the behavior sequences leading to copulation are much more firmly bound to the behaviors of pair formation.

It is conceivable that the sense of values which prompts us to react negatively to the simplification and dissolution of some social norms of behavior, especially the behavior norms of pair formation, is the product of a selection directed toward retention of steadfast norms. But what lies behind our negative valuation of the "ignoble" physical features acquired through domestication and what this should serve is, by way of contrast, completely unclear.

VALUE PERCEPTIONS OF THE JUST AND THE UNJUST

To the crass and flagrant violations of social-behavior norms we respond with an entirely different quality of emotion. The murderer or the ruthless terrorist elicits feelings of horror and deep indignation; we regard them as nonhumans, as monsters or fiends, but certainly not as despicable or "nastily common" people. Contained within the word *common* is the same sense expressed by the word *vulgar*.

On the basis of comparative studies made by members of the team project at Cornell University called "Common Core of Legal Systems," both Peter H. Sand, the American philosopher of law, and Albert Ehrenzweig came to share the remarkable opinion that the feeling a normal human has for what is lawful and right is anchored in an innate, heritable program. They go on to report that in those American states in which a particular crime is covered by especially strict laws and punishable with extremely heavy sentences, jurors demonstrably impose the mildest penalty possible, whereas the reverse is true in those states in which the same crime or offense is covered by milder laws; there the jurors recommend the most severe verdict possible.

Kant's categorical question cannot, curiously, automatically determine if a human behavior pattern originates in a genetic program or in a moral self-interrogation. As is known, the essence of the question can be formulated as follows: can I raise the rules of my conduct to a level of natural law or by doing this, would something contrary to reason result? The negative valuation of the "contrary to reason" is the prerequisite for the answer to the categorical question becoming a commandment, indeed, the categorical imperative, or for the answer becoming a prohibition. The categorical question and an affirming answer to it are often appraised as proof that the human conduct in question is moral, that is, has arisen through the responsibility resulting from reasoning. This is an error easily made. When a child falls into the water and someone jumps in after it and pulls the child out, the maxim, the rule of conduct for this action, can, after the fact, be subjected to the Kantian question and formulated thus: if an adult human sees a child in mortal danger and, without any danger to himself, can rescue the child, he does this. This maxim, raised to a law, contains no reasonable contradiction because the mode of action concerned derives from a genetic program that, in itself, can already qualify as a natural law. Thus a healthy, genetically programmed behavior norm cannot be differentiated from moral behavior by means of the categorical question, even though a genetically programmed behavior norm has come into existence in a far simpler way than any moral action.

All of the norms of human behavior treated in this chapter stand in urgent need of reexamination by means of the Kantian question. The malfunctions of these norms, traceable to the continuously rapidly changing conditions of present-day culture, can be arrested and corrected only through the critical responsibility practiced by humans.

THE VALUES PERCEIVED FOR PROPERTY

As has already been pointed out in an earlier discussion, value perceptions are never a matter of absolute intensities but always only of relative intensities of an experienced quality. And I have already mentioned the relative significance of good and bad. Nevertheless the substantive word "good" does indeed designate a quite specific concept, that of a possession in the form of real property. The word combination "goods and chattels" is just as familiar to us as the adjective "propertied." The word "property" incorporates a conceptualization of enduring residence on a particular piece of land. Among very many animals, possessing territory is certainly genetically programmed. This appears not to be the case for human beings, at least not in their most simple societal forms. Among those cultures which have remained in a hunting-gathering stage, personal, material property apparently plays only a very insignificant role and is certainly most often restricted to material objects of use — utensils, implements, tools and weapons. Such cultures do in fact defend, to a certain extent, the areas through which they move during their more or less regulated system of expeditions and against incursions made by neighboring groups; yet generally speaking, one can assume that a genuine territorial defense first arose hand in hand with agriculture at the same time a hierarchical ordering of society came into being: the division of humanity into lords and laborers.

Killed game as being the property of the hunter was very probably already prescribed among the very early hunting cultures in the form of customary rights arrived at without a great deal of reflection. Of interest to us is the fact that this also applies among chimpanzees. Even a low-ranking chimpanzee which has killed a young pavian or an antelope kid is beseeched, with humbleness, by higher-ranking animals, and generous pieces of the quarry are shared among all the members of the troop, although the distribution cannot be said to proceed "fairly"; preference is shown for friends.

The grazing animals of nomads were, most certainly, a very old form of personal property. The Latin word *pecus*, from which *pecunia* and "pecuniary" are derived, means "small animals"; especially sheep were certainly meant in most cases. Phenomenology can be pursued best by means of self-observation, that is, by describing one's own feelings and hoping that one will be understood by others. Some speculations on my part will, I trust, be permitted. My feelings of joy associated with "having" something involve, as objects, almost exclusively live animals. When by pure accident and without my having assisted or interfered in the matter, a large school of fish matures in an aquarium and then thrives, this gives me a deep sense of satisfaction, even when these fish are, for me, completely uninteresting char. Observing and contemplating our continuously expanding gaggle of graylag geese gives me pleasure, even though we have to do our best to get rid of as many of them as possible in the best way we can, since too large a number makes the overview necessary for our research work too difficult. This self-observation strengthens my opinion that the positive feeling for an increase of the herd and the flock is influenced more by genetic programs than are the other kinds of pleasures perceived for possessions.

A qualitatively different sort of pleasure in having appears to direct itself toward and attach itself to objects that can be collected and accumulated. This pleasure is very heftily released by foodstuffs capable of being kept sufficiently long. The urge to collect objects that are like one another is most probably genetically programmed; it carries within itself the dangerous characteristic that, as the quantity of the already collected objects increases, the strength of the urge also increases. It is known that collectors of particular objects of art can yield to this drive so far that they do not even shy away from criminal actions in order to obtain what they must have. That the rage to collect things can gradually consume the entire personality of the collector, just as a neurosis can, is not something known only to psychiatrists.

One of the most dangerously vicious circles menacing the continued existence of all mankind arises through that grim striving for the highest possible position within the ranked order, in other words, the reckless pursuit of power which combines with an insatiable greed of neurotic proportions that the results of acquired power confer. I have already noted that the quantity of what is collected intensifies the drive to collect; the most evil of the reciprocally augmenting intensities occurs between the acquisition of power and the unquenched thirst for power.

The Question Concerning Nonteleonomically Programmed Value Sensibilities

IS THERE BEAUTY AS SUCH?

For all the value perceptions of humans that have been discussed up to now, the assumption is justified that these sensibilities assist the individual in advantageous achievements and, therewith, the assumption is also justified that their programs as well, through selection of these achievements, have evolved in the typical ways. But there is the beautiful, the genesis of which in a similar manner must be doubted, for which, in fact, an explication of origin by means of selection seems conspicuously contrived. Here we must recall much of what was said in chapter 3 about creative evolution and about *Homo ludens,* the creative human. Humans are indubitably capable of fashioning harmoniousnesses that never existed before and are also capable, at the same time, of perceiving them as well. Perceiving, as Karl Bühler emphasized early on, is also a human activity. In human art there is, without doubt, the beautiful, the existence of which, in the defined sense, is not teleonomic.

Much more difficult to answer is the question why, even at the lower levels of plant and animal life, there is so much for us that is beautiful, that seems to have no apparent species-preserving value. Many butterflies have exceedingly beautiful color designs with innumerable details that are most certainly not seen by conspecifics and cannot frighten enemies away. The markings on the feathers of pheasant hens and on other birds with protective coloring have, when examined closely, very rich colors in well-regulated patterns although the selection pressure that brought these into being was pointed toward making them as similar as possible to the irregular chaotic coloring of the background. Are the colors and patterns as beautiful and orderly as the selection pressure permits? Where the selection pressure favors bright colors and variegated forms that are made even more con- spicuous through their strict regularity, it would seem as if the organisms were "living their lives to the full" as extrav- agant works of art.

Beauty and teleonomic purposefulness are, therefore, not contradictions, but just because, from the point of view of humans, there is genuine beauty in organic nature that ap- pears to possess no teleonomy whatever, it is essential to acknowledge its existence. If one were, however, to account for the fairylike color variegation of marine gastropod mol- lusks as a "self-representation" on the part of the organism, as Adolf Portmann does, one obscures the fact that these creatures, fitted out with stolen nettle capsules, profit from their wealth of color: every voracious enemy who has ever to its detriment attempted to take one of them into its mouth retains their significant colors as an indelible memory.

The problem of the beautiful not bound to a purpose is brought home to me daily by another phenomenon — the song of a bird. E. Tretzel (1965) has written about an achievement that gives us cause for the deepest deliberation.

A crested lark (*Galerida c. cristata L.*) imitated the whistled signals of a shepherd giving commands to his dog. The whistled repetitions of the shepherd were so various that, when plotted over one another by means of sound spectograms, a completely confusing pattern emerged because of "track jumping" and divergent intonations. The lark then presented the following accomplished performance: it transposed the whistled phrases to a higher pitch at which it could more easily produce the sounds and "abstracted" from the vastly varying and, in their intervals, often completely inharmonious whistles of the shepherd those forms which, as Tretzel writes, "come closest to our musical sensibilities. One would almost like to say that the lark had grasped the 'idea,' the ideal Gestalt, of each motif and sang it the way the shepherd had certainly thought it should sound but was only seldom able to produce. Besides this the lark delivered all of the shepherd's whistles much more purely and more musically, more slender in tone and more elegant in the tone sequence. The lark had, so to speak, musically enobled the whistles."

For more than a quarter of a century I have shared my room with shamas, a bird that is, according to my teacher, Oskar Heinroth, and following my own experience, the greatest "artist" of all among the songbirds. The shama (*Copsychus malabaricus*) is usually incorrectly identified as the shama thrush. Johannes Kneutgen has done work on the songs of this bird and their analogy to human art. It is an astonishing fact that these birds produce the most complex and the most beautiful harmonies when *at play*. The singing of all passerine birds has a certain relationship to play, and that much more so the better the species in question is gifted for imitating what it hears. Sitting there at rest with its plumage relaxed, seeming almost sleepy, the bird "plays" with continuously new combinations of mastered sounds. Even these single tones, each one of them beautiful in itself, are dependent on learning processes. M. Konishi has proved that many songbirds can produce no pure tones whatsoever if they have been made deaf early in their lives and have been unable to hear themselves sing.

Just as creative human artistry suffers a significant loss of value when it is made to serve any kind of utilitarian purpose, the song of the shama also loses a tremendous amount of its beauty when, during the defense of its territory or during courtship, the bird becomes very agitated — when, in other words, the bird's song is incorporated as part of a purpose-oriented behavior and made serviceable to that end. Then the bird repeats its loudest and not at all its most beautiful phrases in monotonous succession. With remarkable insight, learning and playing with new combinations of motifs are called by bird devotees "composing." Joachim Ringelnatz sings his praises of the nightingale's song with the words: *"Nur Eins schuf mir Verlegenheit, daß sie dasselbe Schluchzen sang, das schon in der Vergangenheit den Dichtern in die Verse drang. Doch hatten alle Jene recht, die sie besangen, gut und schlecht."* [Just one thing brought me embarrassment, that she sang the same sob which, in the past, penetrated the verses of the poets. Yet all those who sang her praises, good and bad, were right (to do so).] I admit that I find myself sharing the same embarrassment.

THE SENSITIVITY FOR HARMONIES*

A sensitivity for harmonies is most certainly a capacity of that organization of our sense organs and brain structures

---

*Not only the combination of simultaneous musical notes in a chord, nor just the composition, structure, relation and progression of chords, although I certainly mean these, too, but all congruencies, correspondences, consonances and accords that occur for us through the sights, sounds and smells of the world. "Harmoniousness" is very close to what I mean, and I would have continued to use that word in this text (see p. 108) were its sound and form in the plural not so discordant and grotesque.

which we know as Gestalt perception. This not ratiocinated but, in Egon Brunswik's sense, ratiomorphous function is one of the most important forms of perception of humans. Although its mechanisms are not accessible to self-observation, through the work done by Karl Bühler and Egon Brunswik we know enough about these processes in order not to doubt their natural causality. This inaccessibility to self-observation has caused many philosophers to regard Gestalt perception as something originating outside the perceiver. For Goethe it was revelation, for many others "intuition." But in an extraordinary number of ways the functioning of Gestalt perception resembles that of a calculating apparatus. If within physiology or psychology there is a realm for which the calculating apparatus is more than a mere simile, then it is that of Gestalt perception.

Its task is to discover *relationships* that exist among sensory-supplied data or, also, between higher units of perception. This capacity in itself is a minor creative act. The integration of two already existing systemic units, each capable of functioning alone and for itself, into a superordinate system brings into existence a new unit the systemic characteristics of which, until the integration, had simply not existed before. In *Behind the Mirror,* I coined the term "fulguration" for this process, which is characteristic of significant steps in evolution.

Perception is an activity, and the synthesis of two systemic units between which one had previously perceived no relationship corresponds, on the part of our human cognition, quite exactly to an analogous process that takes place in extrasubjective creation. The expression "fulguration" is even more fitting for a progression of thought processes than it is for evolutionary successions. We speak of a "thought flashing" or we say: "It dawned on me" when we succeed in bringing two formerly independent lines of thought into conjunction with each other and then suddenly are confronted by a new way of thinking, by a new system for organizing our thoughts that astonishingly makes cognitive accomplishments possible that were not formerly there.

In one of its capacities, thus, Gestalt perception is at the forefront of human cognition; it is the human mind's forging ahead into the unknown. At the same time it is the warden of the already known, a storer of patiently collected factual material whose substance is many times larger than that which our memory is able to accumulate and keep.

On this capacity the human sensitivities for harmonies also repose, harmonies whose complications are of such immensities that they exceed, by far, the dimensions of anything we are able to comprehend through intellect and reasoning. No wonder the results of Gestalt perception can seem to the human to be a revelation; by means of rational and reasoned thinking the same results could never be achieved.

Gestalt perception is nonetheless no miracle; its thoroughly worldly, mechanical nature shows itself in its need for facts. When these data are insufficient or, in experiments, intentionally falsified, Gestalt perception goes way off the mark. The collection of data is basically a learning process; how indispensable this process is can be demonstrated through the perception of those complex harmonies made accessible to us in musical works of art.

Europe's classical music is known to rest on the foundation of Andreas Werckmeister's *Musical Temperature: clear and mathematical instructions, with the aid of the monochord on how to attain equal temperament in tuning clavier instruments* . . . published in 1691. There Werckmeister set the octave as the only pure interval and divided it into twelve exactly equal semitones, with equalized and tempered individual intervals that provided exactly determined representations of the strict mathematical relationships between oscillation frequencies. Like those acquired for mastering many other complex forms, the perceptions of musical lawfulnesses must also be learned. Sensory data in which the perceivable lawfulnesses prevail must be proffered repeatedly until our perceiving apparatus is capable of comprehending the lawfulnesses in question. From earliest childhood almost all of us have learned to listen for these kinds of harmonies and, for this reason, they seem to us self-evident and unambiguous. Oriental music and also the music heard in North Africa have only whole tones or steps and have, in terms of the mathematical relationships of oscillation frequencies, far stricter laws than Western music. Nevertheless, when we Occidentals hear music in Turkey or in North Africa, we are, at first, completely incapable of extracting its harmonic lawfulness; for us it is chaotic sound and not very melodious. Naturally every Westerner can achieve the capability of perceiving the formal pattern of Oriental music by listening to it repeatedly. Following the "feeding in" of a sufficient amount of data, the Gestalt (as it tends to do in every case) disengages itself from a background of what previously were only chaotic accidentals.

That Orientals are subject to the same processes of learning when listening to our European music is illustrated by a story that was being told when I was still a child. The king of Siam at that time was the guest of Emperor Francis Joseph and was taken to the court opera for a special performance of a Wagner opera in his honor. Afterward, when the Oriental monarch was asked which part of the performance had pleased him most, he answered that this was the rather short piece played at the very beginning of the opera. Further inquiries made clear that he did not mean the overture but the tuning of the instruments.

There are harmonies of quite disparate sorts; our Gestalt perception is capable of perceiving highly complicated polyphonic interactions as harmonies and of reacting to minimal disturbances with a sensitivity similar to that of a conductor discerning the least false tone sounded among the many voices of the orchestra. A person who knows our natural world well and who, through observation and experience, has become familiar with a large number of variegated biotopes in healthy states, can unerringly form an undeliberated but important value judgment: those biotopes are found *beautiful* that are in a balanced ecological equilibrium and can be seen, thus, to be viable for a long time to come. That only tracts of land undisturbed by human intervention can be beautiful is an erroneous stance taken by some romantic environmentalists. What is correct is that where a disturbance of ecological harmonies occurs humans primarily bear the burden of guilt. Even those portions of the earth's solid surface occupied by humans can be beautiful when, in them, an approximation of an ecological communality is sustained. Even those regions whose character is almost completely shaped by human activities can be beautiful, such as some parts of the Rhine Valley with their vineyards, or the billowing grain fields of the Great Plains. What, in contrast, we sense as ugly are the gigantic monocultures in which only a single species of plant covers the entire countryside in every direction all the way to the horizon.

The Relative "Heights" of Harmonies

Although beauty does not allow itself to be quantified, we still sense the value differences between higher and lower harmonies. The organization of a fungus, seen in itself, represents a wonderfully harmonious whole, but when we see a rose plant being devastated by a fungus, we do not hesitate to intervene to the advantage of the higher harmony of the rose. A ciliate with a large nucleus and a small nucleus, with a "silverline" stimulus-conducting system, and with cilia lashes flagellating in a well-regulated tempo arouses our admiration. Yet as soon as we see a fish under attack by one of those parasitic ciliates *Ichthyophthirius,* we perceive the disturbance in the harmony of the host and feel no sympathy for the parasite as we reach for healing medication.

THE PERCEPTION OF PATHOLOGICAL DISTURBANCES

One of the most important accomplishments of Gestalt perception is that of enabling us to differentiate between what is healthy and what is sick. An observer gifted with a reasonable capacity for Gestalt perception who is also sufficiently well acquainted with a particular animal species can simply *see* when something is wrong with one of them. Modern medicine, above all modern medical education and training, generally tends to underestimate enormously the accomplishments of Gestalt perception. It is a mistake to believe that the "clinical eye" or "a nose for pathology" can be completely replaced by any amount of quantifying data and their electronic processing — no matter how indispensable these have become today for its supplementation. I am not referring here at all to the personal relationship between doctor and patient, which I regard as indispensable, but instead to the special circumstances that the doctor faces when participating in the assembly-line system of our large clinics where he can never get to know enough precisely about the individual patient. The family doctor of an earlier tradition who knew each one of his patients as individuals and knew all of the individual characteristics of each had it incomparably easier when making a diagnosis from just the vaguest indication of an illness.

THE REALLY A PRIORI AWARENESS OF VALUE

For all of the perceived values discussed up to this point, harmonies to which our Gestalt perception permits us to respond, it cannot be ruled out entirely that their programs have come into existence phylogenetically — under the selection pressure of accomplishment. It could be an appreciation for harmonies that induces the housewife to struggle against every indication of dilapidation in the house and the garden; when the farmer perceives the slightest disturbance in the health of his animals or his crops, and initiates preventive measures, this could have a teleonomic effect. This general capability could also explain our valuation of the beautiful that is not teleonomic.

I believe, however, that there are value awarenesses which are, in the strictest sense, a priori — not like Immanuel Kant's a priori thought forms and eidetic forms, about which we can assume, with reasonable certainty, that they have evolved during the course of evolution and through interaction with extrasubjective givens. Earlier in this book I expressed the conviction that speculations about those questions we are unable to answer are allowed, and the evolutionary theory of knowledge confirms expressly for us this human right. We know, as has already been stated, that there are innumerable thoroughly natural things and processes which elude the conceptualizing capacities of our *Weltbild-apparat,* and always will remain elusive because they are too complex for its capacities of representation and reproduction. We perceive the unpredictability of what occurs organically as freedom; we perceive creation as having value because we, ourselves, are creative. In our conceptual thinking, processes are at work that are, in many ways, analogous to those of evolution, but probably are only a special case. In the mind of the human there are thought units, ideas, traditions, hypotheses, dogmas and such like, each one of which, in itself, possesses sufficient encapsulation and uniformity in order to come into interaction with one another — not very different from the way in which the various species of living beings have done during the course of evolution. As Karl Popper has said, such units can enter into competition with one another, so that selection plays just as important a role in the realm of knowledge as in the evolution of living beings. About forty years ago I wrote:

> There are . . . innumerable givens in the organic world which lay claim, most intensely, to our positive value judgment and these particular givens have nothing at all to do with species-preserving value. That we, as humans, can respond in the same way to the beauty of a flower, the skeleton of a radiolarian, the song of a bird and a human work of art, derives from determinants which the plant, the radiolarian, the bird and the human, on the basis of coincident structural characteristics inherent in all living protoplasmic forms, what all of them in their essences as living beings have had in common from the very beginning. In this one essentiality of being, immanent in the developmental direction of all organic creation, thinking and being flow . . . together as one [and the same], so that any further substantiation of value judgment is axiomatically impossible. . . . It could very well be that a causal explanation exists for the organic always striving, in all the forms in which it appears, toward the "ever more ordered," why everywhere, whenever species preservation permits this to even a minimal extent, the organic strives toward those "art forms" that once enchanted old Haeckel. I believe the [ultimate] cause for the realization of the harmoniously ordered radiolarian skeleton will . . .

prove to be identical with that which, among humans, has led to the composing of symphonies and to the creation of other works of art. But this knowledge will not disturb the value of these yields of the highest organic creation [; this knowledge] will only tell us why we must judge in one way and not in another. I believe that a structure to which life adheres in its innermost and essential being leads, in humans, to a valuation of values, . . . [that] are, in the most audacious sense of the word[,] "a prioristic" and "thought necessitating," *and not only for human beings but also for all imaginable superhuman beings, provided they have in common with us at least* that *sort of "life" we have in common with protozoa.*

What I wrote with conviction then I still believe to be true today.

At the present time these creative processes finding expression through our perceptions of value are the only ones that still play a significant role on our planet. It is our duty to recognize them as real, to acknowledge them as reality, and to follow them as categorical commands, in the truest sense — to do what they tell us to do.

·⁙ PART THREE Ɪ⁘·

The Mind as Adversary of the Soul

The increasing celerity of developments within our culture and civilization has, as a consequence, that the discrepancy between the social order and the natural inclinations of humans assumes progressively more grotesque forms. "Natural inclinations," in Immanuel Kant's sense, correspond, for the most part, to behavior norms that we regard as genetically programmed; we believe, with William McDougall, that just these "natural inclinations" go hand in hand with qualitatively unmistakable emotions, with what "stirs the soul." The products of collective conceptual thinking, the human mind, show themselves to be the enemy and the adversary of the human soul, and I do not hesitate to borrow from Ludwig Klages, who was the first to recognize this, the title of his book to serve as the heading for the third part of my own book.

Not only genetically programmed norms, but also the norms of human behavior firmly fixated through cultural tradition show themselves to be, in many cases, too "conservative" to be able to adapt to the frenzied pace of change within the modern milieu. A tradition such as patriotism, although not a threat to entire cultures yesterday, can today occasion annihilation.

·◦⟩[SEVEN][◦·

The Uneasiness Inherent in Culture

THE DISCREPANCY OF VELOCITIES

The human soul is very much older than the human mind. We do not know when the soul, all subjective experience, came into being. Every human who is acquainted with higher animals knows that their experiences, their "emotions," are fraternally related to our own. A dog has a soul that, in general, is similar to mine; in its capacity for unconditional love that soul probably even surpasses mine. No animal, however, has a mind in the sense defined here; neither dogs nor the anthropoid apes that are most closely related to humans have such a mind.

The human mind, brought into existence through conceptual thinking, syntactic speech and the heritability of traditional knowledge made possible by speech, develops many times faster than the human soul. As a consequence, humans very often alter their own surrounding world to their disadvantage and to the world's disadvantage. Right now humans are on the verge of destroying the communality of all life on the earth on which and from which they live and, in doing this, committing themselves to suicide.

The rapidity with which the human mind changes and with which the human, through his technology, makes his own world into something completely different from what, just a short while ago, it was, is so great that, for all practical purposes, the pace of evolutionary development, when compared to it, is standing dead still. Since the emergence of human culture the human soul has remained essentially the same; it is not astonishing then that culture very often makes unfulfillable demands on the soul.

In truth a human is, as Arnold Gehlen has said, "by nature a cultural being," that is, even the phylogenetically evolved programs of his behavior are adjusted to the presence of a culture. As Noam Chomsky has made evident, the human possesses an inborn program for logical thinking and for verbal language: the child does not learn how to speak, as Otto Koehler has explained, the child learns only the vocables; the program for verbal language has as a prerequisite that an already extant culture is on hand to provide the child with just these vocables and their significance.

Despite this ready phylogenetic adaptation to the existence of a human culture, the further adaptation of the human cannot keep pace with the increasing speed of changes occurring in civilization and in the social environment; and this discrepancy is becoming greater from year to year.

Culture itself has created norms of human behavior that, in a certain sense, can step in as substitutes for innate behavior programs and as stabilizing, conservative factors place themselves in opposition in order to stem an all too headlong development. There are precepts for behavior prescribed by tradition that have become "second nature" for humans.

Underlying practically all human behavior that presently is "allowed" members of a society is a very extensive network of ritualization known and identified as etiquette. Hans Freyer has shown that the *tenue* forming the foundation of propriety in deportment is not at all just a purely external, superficial and unimportant set of rules for what one can and cannot do; it is also determinative for genuine moral decisions. Not only unritualized, instinctive movements such as scratching oneself, stretching oneself and other actions classified as comfort behavior are forbidden by decorum, by customary "good manners," but also much more complex behavior patterns. These forms of cultural ritualization are something basically different from the commandments for doing and for not doing set by Kantian, responsible self-questioning. Even the sanctions our feelings find to punish us for the two kinds of infraction, the one against the morally analogous demands of decorum and the other against breaches of Kantian morality, are qualitatively different. The punishment for improper behavior is shame; the punishment for immoral behavior is remorse.

The cultural and civilizational straitjacket binding humans today is being drawn tighter and tighter. Neither our natural and creaturely behavior nor the good manners that, traditionally, have become our second nature fit any longer in a world that is artificially contrived and determined almost exclusively by technocracy. My belief is that some youthful rebels confuse these differing constraints, that when protesting against the technocratic/capitalistic success-society they mistakenly violate codes of decorum. It appears to be not understood by some young people that rebellion against the technocratic success-society would have a much greater chance of success if they could refrain from offenses against propriety, honor and aesthetic-ethical convention. Nevertheless, all the rebellions staged by today's youth, even when they are not always thought through thoroughly, signify the presentiment of a truth: the human mind, in taking us down the path of technocracy, has become the adversary of life itself and collaterally the adversary of the human soul.

INCLINATION AND MORALITY

In the Bible it is written that the imagination of man's heart is evil from his youth. As stated above, we feel different sorts of discomfiture when we act contrary to the laws of morality and when we act contrary to the laws governing behavior firmly laid down through cultural ritualization. When within the context of good manners we have behaved badly, we feel at the most shame, although this can be felt very intensely. In our civilization, transgressions against ritual custom arouse from uninvolved observers more laughter and commiseration than indignation.

Infractions against morality, as taught by the Ten Commandments, call up other feelings. Instead of shame, the offender feels remorse; the uninvolved observer, however, feels indignation. A normal human being follows these commandments from natural inclination — when his behavior involves *personal friends.* One does not lie to a friend or steal from a friend, and one does not covet a friend's wife; least of all does one kill a friend. The Ten Commandments begin to lose their fundamental effectiveness when the anonymity of human society increases.

Remarkably, Immaneul Kant assigns no value at all to natural inclination. For deeds done through natural inclination one can claim no moral merit, not even when the action taken is thoroughly altruistic and socially praiseworthy. The notable spinelessness of this standpoint taken by one of our greatest philosophers provoked the ridicule of one of our greatest poets. Friedrich Schiller parodied it with this epigram: *"Gerne dien' ich dem Freund, doch leider tu ich's aus Neigung, darum wurmt es mich oft, daß ich nicht tugendhaft bin. . . . Drum lerne den Freund zu verachten, um dann mit Abscheu zu tun, was die Pflicht dir gebeut."* [I like helping a friend, but unfortunately I do this from inclination; for this reason it often irks me that I am not virtuous. . . . Therefore learn to despise the friend, so that you can do with aversion, what duty demands of you.]

For Kant the only morally meritorious ways of behaving are those that are planned in anticipation of their consequences. Kant's categorical question can be abbreviated as follows: Can I raise the maxim of the action I am planning to the level of a natural law, or would such action emerge as opposed to reason? Translated into the language of biological sociology, the question can be worded thus: Is the planned action teleonomic, that is, species-preserving and society-preserving, or not?

Hence the categorical question is not suitable for differentiating genetically programmed inborn motivations from motivations arrived at by reasoning. When, acting on pure instinct, responding to a drive motivation, I shield a dear friend from exposure to danger and afterward ask myself the categorical question about being able to raise the maxim of this action to the level of a natural law, the answer to the question quite obviously has to be "Yes" because it already is a natural law.

But genetically programmed inclinations of humans are not sufficient for coping with the social demands of a modern society comprising millions of individual members. Within a group of humans who are friends or acquaintances almost everyone will uphold the Ten Commandments. Each one will, as well, unhesitatingly expose himself to a good deal of danger, even place his own life on the line, to rescue a friend from danger. An American sociologist has calculated that the optimal number for a group bound by close friendship is eleven. One cannot avoid making the association that eleven is the number on a team for so many games and that of Jesus' twelve disciples only eleven remained loyal.

The imagination of the human heart is not evil from youth onward; humans are good enough for eleven-man societies, but not good enough to commit themselves for an anonymous, personally unknown member of a mass society, as they would be willing to do for an individual personally known and for someone who is a close friend. The social commandments as well as the social proscriptions that have arisen during the course of cultural development force us constantly to do violence to the innate programs of our behavior; in concourse with other members of society we are continuously restrained by the straitjacket of cultural behavior norms.

The higher a culture develops, that much greater becomes the tension between human inclination and cultural demand. Not one person living in our culture is free from inner tensions. In today's industrial states there are already dangerously large numbers of people no longer capable of compensating for this tension and who become either asocial or neurotic. One can, accordingly, define the psychically disturbed as those who either suffer themselves or make society suffer.

No one is exempt from suffering. The healthy can be differentiated from the sick only analogously, as a person with a compensated heart ailment can be differentiated from another sick person whose compensation has broken down. From this emerges a solution to the pseudoproblem raised by the contradiction in the positions taken by Immanuel

Kant and Friedrich Schiller cited above. None of us is "good enough," every one of us would be brought into conflict with the demands of our cultures and societies were he to follow his instincts blindly. But the outfitting with social instincts, especially with social inhibitions, is uncommonly variable from person to person. To remain with the example of the compensated and uncompensated heart ailments: the one has more to be compensated for, the other less. When I judge human individuals as *being* good or less good, I quite obviously esteem highest those who are good to me and helpful to me out of friendship and pure inclination, and not those who, under extreme self-control, behave toward me, objectively seen, in the same way. If, on the other hand, I judge the *actions* of an individual (my own, for example), then those appear to me to be praiseworthy that I do because of Kantian morality and carry out despite my clearly discernible disinclinations.

In what has just been outlined is contained the truth of all the sermons on asceticism, but also the danger to be found in behaviorism and the stimulus-response model that presents animals as well as humans as sheer reactive apparatuses reacting only to stimuli, as if to pressed buttons, and possessing no spontaneity of their own. Actually, a majority of the instinctive programs of humans and of animals are based on spontaneous stimulus production. Stimuli surge up with great force and become dangerous when the adequate situation for their release fails to appear. Sigmund Freud deserves a great deal of credit for having recognized this danger. At a time when the Sherringtonian reflex theory was regarded as the last word of wisdom and had found the readiest acceptance within behaviorism and stimulus-reaction psychology, Freud recognized the fundamental fact of spontaneity in the life of drives, in instinctive behavior.

With splendid simplicity he gathered together and subsumed, under the concept of Eros, all of the life-sustaining and species-preserving instincts.

Cultural developments appear to concern themselves remarkably little with the well-being of individuals. Human rights, that is, human needs arising from the innate dispositions of individual humans that must be satisfied, appear to have little influence on the developmental directions of cultures. The power that is exercised by tradition and by the formation of traditional rites appears to know no bounds. One is appalled when one learns what cruelties and repressions the undoubtedly high culture of the Incas could contrive without inciting a rebellion among the masses.

When we consider the renunciations of fundamental human rights freely undertaken by the people forming today's industrial societies, we must ask ourselves if we have any essential advantage over the Inca culture: the stress to which members of all strata of our society are exposed is increasing steadily. The concept of stress (taken over directly as *Streß* by German speakers and used as part of everyday speech) designates each and every encumbrance the organism must bear. An encumbrance is present not only when a human being is overtaxed by all the coercive forces already cited, but also when the challenges and the variety offered him are insufficient.

··⊰[EIGHT]⊱··

Malfunctions of
Once-Meaningful
Behavior Patterns

THE DEFINITIONS OF NORMAL AND PATHOLOGICAL

Ultimately, all of the culturally disturbing processes that must be discussed in this chapter are caused by the discrepancy between the rates of cultural development and of genetic evolution. The conceptualized pairs — healthy and sick, normal and pathological — can be defined only from a stance that views them teleonomically, that is, only in relation to the increased or decreased chances for survival an organism acquires in a particular environment from the characteristic that is to be judged. A classic example for such a relative judgment is the condition known as sickle-cell anemia, a heritable malformation of the red blood cells that considerably disturbs blood oxygenation but, at the same time, makes the red blood cells immune to attack by the trypanosomes causing malaria. In Gambia, before the beginning of this century, almost all of the "healthy" people were those who suffered from sickle-cell anemia since most of the people with normal blood cells had died as children from the endemic, severe form of malaria.

Thus what is normal and what is pathological cannot be distinguished in every case by means of precise definitions. Yet I still want to discuss in what follows two separate kinds of malfunctions: on the one hand, those that are activated by behavior programs originally teleonomic for human society and only within the environmental circumstances of the present day are ruinous for mankind; and, on the other hand, those that clearly bear the character of the morbid and, exactly as neuroses by definition do, become "overvalued"; that is, the personality of the sick person is overwhelmed to an extent that all other motivations are suppressed completely. We should not forget that through its potent capacity for inheriting culturally acquired characteristics, our species was enabled, initially, to be uncommonly successful biologically. Like no other vertebrate form before it, the species has become the "characteristic fossil" during its own continuing era. More than anything else, this colossal success has conjured up the dangers that threaten us today.

Not just a few of the behavior norms to be discussed in this chapter have been, until a very short time ago, clearly useful for mankind and therefore qualify even today, not entirely unjustifiably, as virtues. Under existing circumstances, however, they tend to hyperfunction, bringing dangerous consequences in tow. (Here I want to recall the already cited research strategy of Ronald Hargreaves, who, when examining any behavioral disturbance of humans, habitually began with the question whether, perhaps, the problem was an overfunctioning or an underfunctioning of an otherwise healthy and teleonomic behavior pattern.)

LOVE OF ORDER AND OVERORGANIZATION

There can be no doubt that a love of order is originally a programming of behavior and can be numbered among the human virtues. It is closely interwoven with the value we sense for harmonies, for the healthy, coordinated interaction we perceive among the elements of an organic system. Aldous Huxley says, "The wish to impose order upon confusion, to bring harmony out of dissonance and unity out of multiplicity, is a kind of intellectual instinct, a primary and fundamental urge of the mind." In the realm of natural science research the wish to impose order is indispensable, but it is also accompanied by certain dangers. The urge to formulate a unified view of the world has misled many scientists into making forced constructions of systems that are "explanatively monopolistic." Just as important, understandably, is the negative evaluation that wells up in us when organic wholenesses break apart, whenever there is disorder and chaos.

In the course of mankind's history the desire for order did not become a danger until quite late. Given the conditions and circumstances of the oldest hunting and gathering groups, the organization of human society would not have been much more complicated than that, say, of a wolf pack, a chimpanzee horde, an elementary school class. Although in these groups a clear rank order among the individuals does in fact exist and can actually lead at times to a tyranny of the strongest or, worse, to the formation of a "clique" of the higher ranking members and therewith to a repulsive oppression of the weaker ones, this tyranny is still neither genetically programmed nor traditionally institutionalized. One does not know for certain in which form an institution of social classes first came into being, but suggesting itself is a connection between such stratification and the emergence of individual *property*. If not already established earlier among nomadic peoples, then an institutionalized rank ordering among individuals began later in our culture with permanent agricultural settlements. The economy of farming was certainly initially organized as a family endeavor: father, mother, sons and daughters of various ages were each provided with certain rights and duties firmly established by tradition. For that land in which one had invested a great deal of work one naturally raised claims to rights of possession, and from this followed a traditionally defined right of inheritance. The oldest son inherited, the younger sons without property went to work for their brother or for other farmers, and in this way the institution of the farm laborer, the employee, came into being. As Freyer has convincingly demonstrated, with the establishment of permanent agricultural settlements animosity arose toward nomads since, naturally, a farmer did not look on serenely while a nomad drove his herds onto the cropland the farmer had cultivated with so much difficulty. Perhaps the biblical fratricide is a symbolic representation of this animosity. As a child, I often wondered how it could have happened that Cain, a tiller of the ground, killed Abel despite the fact that Abel, as a herdsman, a keeper of sheep, was surely much better versed in the slaughtering of larger creatures than was his brother, the caretaker of "the fruits of the ground."

The origin of castes or classes in human society was doubtless associated with the institutionalization of private ownership, whether this involved animals or land. However all this may have been, it was the tilling of soil that had two dangerous consequences: the first was that land cultivators became quite certainly far more aggressive in the defense of their fields than groups of hunters and bands of gatherers among whom territorial aggression played no vitally important role. If territorial aggressivity was subsequently intensified through cultural tradition or if, over a very long period of time (and long periods of time are what concern us here), a genetical modification in human aggressivity occurred, we do not know. The second dangerous consequence of settled agriculture was that it made possible an explosive increase in the earth's human population.

One should not, however, imagine the first stages of the hierarchical organization of a human group as being all that hard and cruel. If we can trust Homer, whose realistic presentations of interpersonal behavior appear to me to be highly credible, then the relationships between the master and the retainer, even those between the owner and the slave, were most "familiar." One remembers the friendship that existed between Odysseus and the slave his father had purchased, the swineherd Eumaios. The kings on the small island of Ithaca, and there seem to have been several, were apparently not much more than farmers having large landholdings; nevertheless they were empowered to lead their subjects into battle. Being led into battle led to the taking of captives and, since these did not belong to the kin group of the conqueror, to slaves in the actual sense of the word.

With an increase in the population the larger landholdings became kingdoms; the familiar relationship, knowing one another at all personally, diminished, lost its significance, and this knowing one another is, as we have learned, the most important dissipater of aggressivity. For just this reason is the depersonalization of interhuman relationships as they now exist in our society so dangerous. With an increase in population the numerical relationship between rulers and ruled was also shifted. Such shifting is, as we shall see, a predictable consequence of the size of societies, and not distinctive to the feudal social order alone. Yet in the feudal form its effect is particularly revolting when the few who rule wallow arrogantly in luxury and profusion while a huge majority of the ruled vegetate in misery. The tyranny of feudal rulers led to the French Revolution among other things. The beautiful words *Liberté, Egalité, Fraternité* appear at first to preface a new epoch in the history of mankind — even if the invention of the guillotine allows us to be a bit doubtful.

It must be the goal of democracy to arrive at a compromise between maintaining the order that a gigantic number of people make absolutely necessary and preserving those freedoms for individual action which belong to the rights of man. Achieving this high goal through legislation is much more difficult than most honest democrats are willing to admit. Even if the effectiveness of democracy were not undermined by the power of large industries at work behind the scenes, there would still remain the virtually insurmountable difficulties of converting, in a just way, what the voters most desire into the actions taken by those for whom they have voted. Large populations mean that there are too many voters and too few people to be voted for. Even within a morally irreproachable, truly democratic government too much power is concentrated in the hands of a very few people. Very few people, however intelligent and morally faultless they may be, are capable of preserving their whole humaneness once they are in positions of power. The delusions of a Caesar are symptoms of a very real illness.

In an industrial society an increase of what is owned also signifies an increase of power; this cannot be prevented. In our mass-society world with a free enterprise economy it is inevitable that smaller business ventures with their limited capital will lose out in competition with larger companies.

It is clear that with the continued advances of technology, the largest producers will eventually control everything. It is an error to believe that the world is governed by politicians. Behind them stand the real tyrants, the large manufacturing corporations. When the armament race continues on both sides of the iron curtain despite all summit meetings and disarmament talks, this happens not because the Russians and the Americans fear each other but because industry *profits* thereby.

Together with the continued advances of technology has gone a commensurate development in the organization of human society. Complicated social organizations had to be devised to complement and accommodate the complicated machinery. They were necessary so that the production apparatus could run smoothly and without friction. In order to fit themselves into this organization, individuals have to become de-individualized. In order to fulfill exactly specified functions, they must make themselves over into automatons. Millions of completely "normal" humans live frictionlessly in a society against which they should, if they were really to stand on their rights as humans, revolt. Although they continue to uphold the illusion of their individuality, they have already actually relinquished a great part of their freedom. Their continued assent to the present social order can only lead imperceptibly to a further loss of individuality.

The vaster the number of people who must be kept in order, that much more rigid will be the necessary organization set over them to accomplish this, and that much more pernicious its dehumanizing effect. The growth of industry draws together increasingly larger portions of the ever-increasing number of humans into the ever-expanding cities, and this is not healthy. We know that mental illnesses, drug addiction and criminality correlate with the concentration of humans in large cities. Paradoxically, a glimmer of hope is discernible in the fact that humans are not yet sufficiently dehumanized genetically to fit themselves into the homogenizing process without suffering damage. Erich Fromm says: "Our contemporary Western society, in spite of its material, intellectual and political progress, is increasingly less conducive to mental health, and tends to undermine the inner security, happiness, reason and the capacity for love in the individual; it tends to turn him into an automaton who pays for his human failure with increasing mental sickness, and with despair hidden under a frantic drive for work and so-called pleasure." Fromm sees grounds for hope in the neurotic symptoms appearing among the people who live in cities; "where there are symptoms there is conflict, and conflict always indicates that the forces of life which strive for integration and happiness are still fighting." The human continues the struggle against his dehumanization; many people appear to be "normal" only because the humane voice within them has been struck dumb.

In order to loosen the superorganizational hold on the mass of humans alive today, a fundamental restructuring of human society is necessary — in other words, a devaluation of many of the value concepts determining what happens in our world today. Obviously this cannot but involve great dangers. Especially at the present time, when all of us have experienced disruptions and wars and can see these continuing in many parts of the world, the anxiety brought on by the thought of chaos appears to dictate that we should acquiesce unconditionally to the organization existing now. The love of order can turn humans into tyrants, and some despots have thus been able to seize power only because a majority of the people entertained the hope that they would be imposing order on a "disordered state of affairs."

THE PLEASURE EXPERIENCED THROUGH INCREASE

Humans enjoy witnessing growth and augmentation. A farmer is happy when his grain crop is growing well, when he can acquire a new field or add on to his house, when his herds show gratifying increases. I can still remember clearly that as children we were proud and pleased when our village grew larger, that we visited every new house being built and how we found each such new construction to be an asset. This has changed completely. The insight that a too large house, a too large business or proposed project, is not more beautiful and better than one of modest proportions is beginning to make headway. If one voices this insight, one often hears in reply from people in business that growth, and moreover exponential growth, is something quite natural and, for this reason, is also a legitimate phenomenon for any human undertaking. It is a fact that even a little fir tree grows "exponentially"; indeed, it grows in all directions simultaneously, that is, spatially, and thereby in rough approximation cubically. In my comparison of biological and economic growth I refer to individual plants only and disregard completely their reproduction through seed; in the natural world there is actually no example of purely linear growth.

The growth of a plant and that of an industrial or commercial enterprise have a lot in common. Both grow, as already stated, exponentially, and both find it very difficult to stop that growth for even a short period of time. That plants are able to intersperse longer rest pauses, such as our deciduous trees do during winter and many desert plants do during the dry seasons, is the result of a particular adaptation. Metabolism can be reduced to a minimum; the organism can exist for long periods "on the back burner" without any energy intake. A commercial enterprise can do this, too, but not as well since the invested capital pitilessly demands a constant return.

Still, more important than the similarities are the differences between the living systems here compared. Unlike Jack's beanstalk, trees do not grow through the clouds on up into the heavens. Evolutionary fixed limits for natural aging do not exist for nothing; purely physical circumstances, such as the increasing difficulty of transporting liquids, the pressure of the wind, among many others, limit the extent of growth. A human enterprise, in contrast, is potentially immortal; not only is no limit set to its growth, it is in fact that much less subject to disruption the larger it becomes. Multinational concerns have not been known to go into bankruptcy. Karl Marx predicted with complete accuracy that, as a consequence of the greater tenacity of the larger corporations, their continued growth would gradually push all smaller enterprises to the wall and reduce them to a state of financial ruin. More than all others, the smallest entrepreneurs, the independent artisans, seem condemned to dying out. Some recent indications that this development might have been stopped, even reversed, provides some ground for optimism.

A further important difference between the growth of a plant and that of a commercial enterprise is that, in the course of its individual life, a plant is not able to alter its means of "earning income." When the materials necessary for its growth have gradually been reduced, it can only grow more slowly, and when it has completely exhausted its sources of nourishment, it must die. But an industrial enterprise improves its methods continually. When the number of whales decreases, the techniques for their capture become more refined. That this must lead in the clearly foreseeable future to a complete exhaustion of the source appears to be a matter of indifference to the whaling industry. Large concerns will most certainly not be wiped out when oil resources are gradually depleted; their capacities for self-regulation are too great for this to happen. The giant corporations, the "multis," are already in control of a vast part of the commercial world. The monopolies of powerful capitalists force mankind to bow before the tyranny of the "experts" who, themselves confined through specialization within particular professional spheres, in turn subject themselves obediently to the dictates of the monetary experts.

In *Brave New World* and *Brave New World Revisited,* Aldous Huxley has outlined a dismal picture of a future in which the species *Homo sapiens* does in fact survive and does develop a stable system ensured against all dangers but in which being human is not possible since all humaneness has disappeared.

Hope that the fate of mankind can be set and then held in another direction still remains. But if this is what we want to happen, human morals and mankind's sense of values must be allowed to conquer the almost irresistible tendencies of phylogenetically programmed behavior. The joy and pleasure derived from the increase of one's possessions are not the only motivations driving us humans toward ruin. Other powerful instinctive programs — the lust for power, the striving for status — all are forcing us in the same direction. The recognition that an undertaking of moderate size is desirable, that a decentralization of the means of production is absolutely necessary, that a constant increase in national economic growth is unrealistic and must be brought to a halt, is desperately difficult to realize when it is up against the technocratic system that is dominating the world today.

In one particular case the urge toward growth and increase of large enterprises, the drive toward consolidation and the subsequent elimination of smaller endeavors, has had especially evil effects; this concerns the communications media, particularly the newspapers. Jefferson, that grand optimist, greeted in his time the burgeoning of newspapers and believed that when everyone could read and if the newspapers were allowed to print everything they wanted to, the general knowledge all citizens would thus have in common could only compel a concurrence of opinion among them. Jefferson lived long enough to witness and realize that freedom of the press can be exploited for the dissemination of lies. Because newspapers and periodicals, just like manufacturing corporations, are inclined to grow and to consolidate, a continual reduction of independent opinion is going on in publishing in the Western world until finally the print media will become concentrated within the empires of only a very few who are attentive to the wishes of the greatest industrial concerns. Here, too, quantitative growth marks an end to creative evolution.

THE JOY OF FUNCTIONING

Another programmed norm of human behavior that in its original form is a blessing for mankind but that, within the circumstances and conditions of an overorganized mass society, can become a curse is the wish to be active, the desire to function that Karl Bühler called *Funktionslust.*

Living beings capable of carrying out very complex and accomplished movements, that is, creatures capable of learning systems of purposeful movements they can choose to perform or not perform, produce such movements with pleasure. The sequence of movements originally directed toward a particular purpose becomes an end in itself, as H. F. Harlow, among others, has shown. In experiments with rhesus monkeys he placed a lure inside a crate sealed with a lock; the lure could be reached only by opening the lock. After the monkeys had learned the difficult operations involved in opening various locks, they took such pleasure in this activity that locks themselves could later be used as inducements for the learning of other behavior patterns.

Every accomplished movement executed well provides pleasure even when the sequence has been mastered under very adverse circumstances and was acquired grudgingly. Very many learned movements are performed by humans for the sake of the movements themselves, and often accompanied by an outlay of large sums of money — golfing, skiing, in fact, almost every sport. One can only say, quite generally, that the more difficult a system of movements is to learn that much more joy its function provides.

The joy of functioning is also a blessing for the working human. Everyone who can do something well takes pleasure in executing the accomplished movements involved. A carpenter talking about the wood he is working might say something like: "It planes as easily as butter smears," and he can express himself with as much enthusiasm as a skier telling about an ideal slope covered with powder snow. Without this joy in capabilities and accomplishments the workday world of humans would naturally be much grayer and much less bearable.

The joy of functioning can also extend to the utilization of complicated machines, even to purely mental applications, or tie itself into such operations. People who have a talent for numbers take pleasure in making rapid and accurate calculations. This pleasure in calculating can also be the pleasure experienced when operating a calculating machine and when working with a computer. Here other factors come into play as well; one can say that the presence of a computer, the utilization of a computer, has now become a scientific and a commercial status symbol. I have often experienced the way in which young scientists who are learning to use computers react to these electronic machines — like small boys who are being introduced to their first electric trains. It is most certainly methodologically correct and procedurally healthy for a modern natural scientist who is dependent on quantification to get the best training possible and the most thorough knowledge of what calculating machines can do, since he can then use them to good purpose. Unfortunately, however, the fun of playing around with computers can make itself just as independent as other activities do under the influence of the functioning pleasure. Then the use of computers is no longer a means to an end but becomes part of an end in itself. In other words, the young scientist will begin to prefer projects that can only be carried out, by design, through copious use of a computer.

The great danger accompanying the *Funktionslust* into the technocratic era is that pleasure-accentuated actions and activities soar to the heights of becoming ends in themselves. What has just been said about the use of computers applies to the entire apparatus set up for production and manufacture.

The Joy of Competition

It is certainly a genetically programmed form of behavior of humans that someone good at doing something strives to exceed someone else in that activity. Even among the higher animals there are analogous behavior patterns. Here the behavior in question involves primarily forms of ritual fighting such as the so-called mouth pulling done by parti-colored perch (Cichlidae), among which some forms, such as *Hemichromis bimaculatus,* also engage in a sort of speed competition that Alfred Seitz has termed the "parallel gallop." Just as among these particolored perch, the swimming races of *Zanclus canescens* described by William Beebe are also a form of ritualized behavior that has, without doubt, derived from fighting movements. Everyone has seen young dogs racing around and the galloping fleetness of young hoofed animals, especially competent at escaping, for which chasing and being chased is the most frequent form of play. H. Hediger has drawn attention to the fact that, among herbivorous "flight animals," it is the one being chased, and among carnivorous animals it is the one doing the chasing that, in each case, is the animal putting its heart into the contest. From an assortment of games played by humans, competitions arise that often take on many of the characteristics of a battle. It is regrettable that through this process so very many forms of sport have been progressively deprived of their joyous, playful character and, through this process, have not only lost their stress-alleviating function but have themselves become a prime source of excessive stress. No friend to animals would subject any animal to the excruciating exertions children with talent for sport are made to undergo. As a physician I would like to intervene at once whenever I observe the complete exhaustion visible in the expression and bearing of young skaters who have just finished performing in competition their programs of free figures.

Hardly any aspect of human life is exempt from competitive efforts and their influence. What was once a thoroughly useful and stimulating factor among prehuman creatures, and even at the lower cultural levels humanity once occupied, has become, with a rise in the cultural level and with a population increase, a menace. When two closed groups of humans begin to compete with each other, collective aggressivity can, under certain circumstances, be augmented by enthusiasm (to be discussed below), and this combination contributes to an escalation of any contest. In the end the irresistible tendency to compete could very well culminate in the collective suicide of mankind.

DIVISION OF LABOR AND SPECIALIZATION

The coming into being of conceptual thinking and verbal language signified a new capability for acquiring and storing information in a way analogous to that which, until then, the immensely old life functions of mutation and selection had been doing this. Since knowledge generates knowledge, cultural development accelerates. An accumulation of the collective knowledge of mankind thus surpasses, and in rapidly increasing dimensions, the capacity for knowledge of a single human brain. This means that a division of knowledge among individual humans cannot be avoided. A division of labor is a completely normal organic process. Very early on, among the protozoa, nucleus and cytoplasm are separate and fulfill diverse functions. The same principle applies for all multicellular animals, and the more differentiated the parts become, naturally that much more dependent they become upon one another and upon their integral entirety as an organism. An earthworm can be cut into several pieces, each of which is capable of surviving, but already at the level of development a centipede has achieved, survival does not occur when the centipede is cut in half.

During Leonardo da Vinci's time it was probably still

possible for one person to know almost everything worth knowing in his immediate world. Today the situation is different. Each individual is able to master only a small part of all the knowledge accumulated by mankind and this small part becomes smaller and smaller every year. In addition, the overorganization of urban civilization with its pernicious competition forces a pace of such haste that the human is hardly allowed time for mastering what he must know and be able to do in order to be capable of competing within his job or profession. While still quite young, one must now decide on a particular direction of study or on a special branch of work and what one is given to learn takes up so much time that no leisure is left, nor any energy, for pursuing possible interests in other areas of knowledge. Least of all does one have time to think, to contemplate, to reflect. Reflecting, however, turning things over in the mind, is a constituent, an essential activity for mankind, and the freedom that one needs for this is a human right.

The pressure to specialize not only restricts the horizons of humans, it also makes the world awfully boring. It is my firm conviction that the "depletion of meaning" occurring in our world, about which Viktor Frankl has said so much that is pertinent, is to a considerable extent a consequence of specialization. If one loses an overall view of the world as a whole, or if one has never achieved such a perspective, one can also not know or one ceases to discern how beautiful and interesting the world is.

Among those Eskimo who have not been in continuous contact with other cultures every man is capable of fulfilling all of the functions that, in his tribe, are necessary. He can fish, spear seals, construct an igloo or a sled. Within our Western culture a division of labor is mentioned early and in the most ancient myths. Apollo did not make his own harp, Hermes made it for him by stealing an armored shell from the turtle and the horns from a goat. In both the Greek myths and the Nordic sagas there is a blacksmith of the gods who limps. What can be more plausible than the assumption that a strong man who has been crippled in an accident and can no longer go along on the hunt and on war expeditions should turn his attention to the making of weapons and other objects and can soon do this so well that his specialization becomes "profitable" for him as well as for his society?

Very likely this form of "manufacturer" existed quite early. At the time when metals were first coming into use probably not every member of a tribe was capable of casting and forging a sword blade or a spear point. Nowadays hardly anyone is still in a position of being able himself to produce any object that is in daily use. I myself could fabricate neither the felt-tip pen I have in my hand nor the glasses resting on my nose; the metal hinges, the glass lenses and the plastic frames of the glasses have certainly been finished by three human specialists (or factory machines).

Although I am not capable of producing the various parts of my spectacles myself, I still have some insight into their physical functions and I am able, in an emergency, to put them back into some kind of working order by making primitive repairs involving wire and isolation tape.

The more complex pieces of utility equipment designed for human use become, that much less insight has the consumer into their function. The electronics of my color television set I do not understand even approximately. This last example illustrates that a complete lack of insight on the part of the consumer does not prevent his using this instrument designed by a specialist with the highest intelligence and with a gift for invention. The more specialized this intelligence, that much less can insight into the way the machine works be expected; the machine must be made completely foolproof.

A division of labor and specialization are, in themselves, nothing pathological. But what in the development of human society is different from what occurs in the evolution of an organism, and is threatening, is the excessive competition among the parts that form the entirety of human society. There is no competition among the organs of an organism, but an automobile factory is in competition with other automobile factories, although the automobiles of every factory have the same function as "organs" of locomotion or as locomotory prostheses for humans. What is happening here in technological areas unfortunately has compelling parallels in the area of general human intellectual accomplishments. In no way different from the technical constructor, the scientist is also forced to extremes of specialization if he wants to remain capable of competing at all. He simply has no time left over to concern himself with other special areas that are not in his immediate field. It would in fact be resented were he to try to do this; he would be accused of unscientific dilettantism and he would be confronted with the old saying that Hans Sachs has long since refuted: "Cobbler, stick to your last."

A state of affairs in which no specialist possesses sufficient knowledge about what his neighbors are doing has the inevitable consequence that everyone regards his own special field as the most important of all and this, in turn, leads to a dangerous dislocation within one's consciousness of reality. "Real" for every human is what he interacts with every day, that with which he must come to terms during his work day. Because in their daily rounds a majority of humans come in contact only with inanimate objects and primarily with things that humans themselves have produced, they come to have an exaggerated conception of what is *possible* for humans *to do*. They have lost the necessary respect for (above all, the sobering perspective that includes) what humans are *not* capable of doing or making; they have forgotten how to behave and associate with living things, with the entire communality of all that is alive, all that in which and with which and from which we humans live.

The Enforced Abstention from Insight

The overrating of one's own restricted area of knowledge does not prevent one specialist from granting another specialist unlimited authority. Each specialist is forced to do this since it is impossible for him to have formed his own opinion about an area of specialization unknown to him. As I have already stated, all of us constantly use tools, machines and equipment whose ways of functioning we do not completely comprehend and which we are unable to produce ourselves.

This abstention from insight is inevitable. The consumer who uses a machine whose inner workings he does not understand must follow exactly the directions for use that the manufacturer has enclosed with his product. The more complicated the product, that much less insight into its functioning on the part of the user must be presumed by the manufacturer; automation must replace insight; the sound or sight signals a machine sends the user as commands must be made simpler and simpler. On the dashboard where, not so long ago, automobiles still had an oil-pressure indicator in the form of a manometer, today most models have nothing more than a red light that warns the driver when something is not in order with the oil circulation.

Specialists in all areas must make it a habit to accept

without question the opinions of other specialists and to depend on them. This opens the door for a new area of specialization, a new profession: that of advertising.

ADVERTISING

This, too, in itself, is nothing evil, nor is it nonbiological. Even the robin sitting at the top of a tree singing loudly and showing its beautiful red breast reflecting the sunlight is advertising itself. Every courting and displaying bird or fish does the same thing. All the so-called imposing displays that are initiated in order to impress, such as, for example, the marvelous *piaffe,* the collected trot of a stallion executed in place, are simultaneously intended as an intimidation of competing males and an advertisement for the sake of a female. As I will discuss more completely in a later chapter on the lie and its evil consequences, the information disseminated by an animal advertising is absolutely reliable: the robin with the most beautiful red breast and the loudest song really is, also in every other regard, the best.

Humans are also allowed to advertise and must, in fact, do this. A scientist is obligated, in what he says and through what he writes, to pass on what he has learned and to spread this knowledge as widely as possible. One expects him to inform in a truthful manner and to convince by means of reasonable argumentation. This manner and these means are, in every respect, allowed. When an automobile firm announces that its latest model has four-wheel drive, there is nothing to be said against this pronouncement of fact; this is true for all advertising communicating facts about products. But current advertising is not much concerned with facts and uses quite specific techniques intended primarily for the feelings of the consumer; there is not even the suggestion of an attempt to provide the consumer with some comprehensible insight into the structure and the capacities of the product being praised.

Especially in a society whose political system is democratic, the public should also be absolutely and honestly informed about the pros and cons of every question. This requirement can be fulfilled, however, only if the public is able to understand this information. For this requisite understanding, the specialization and the associated limitations to single areas of knowledge I have just spoken about pose difficult obstructions to be got over. Today's civilized human feels himself to be competent only in his own special field and is actually relieved when he can feel exempted from responsibility for problems not involving his area of specialization, although some of the problems are those that remain the concern of everyone generally. He is in some cases even ready, unfortunately, to buy political opinions as prefabricated finished products, and various producers of opinion are, accordingly, prepared to provide him with these wares, for which they make propaganda in exactly the same way producers advertise their consumer goods.

Using the methodology of the natural sciences, advertising specialists have discovered that it is a mistake to approach the public they want to reach on a basis that appeals to reason. It is far more advantageous, they have learned, to address themselves to the deep-seated feelings, to the emotionality located at the unconscious levels of the human soul. It is not effective at all to lecture scientifically, desiring to teach; the head of an advertising agency is successful when he understands how to manipulate instincts and emotions. Whoever wants to win over great masses of human beings uses "keys to their hearts," gains access to the unconscious levels of their minds. There the genetically programmed behavior norms sit — fear, the sexual drive, the urge to get ahead, to climb socially — that can be manipulated with the help of coldly calculated, supernormal releasers. Practically all of the instinctive feelings and emotions can be appealed to in this way through propagandistic measures. In doing this it is most essential, as Aldous Huxley correctly states, that the addressee remains unaware of the fact that he is being presented only with a symbol of his wishes and not with their fulfillment. An advertisement for a bathing suit or for a skin cream appears to promise that the fortunate woman making the purchase will look exactly like the photographer's model used by the advertiser. The producers of cosmetics sell, as Huxley reports one such manufacturer's saying, "not lanolin, but hope." Lanolin is cheap; for the hope part, however, the producer is prepared to be paid an extremely high price.

The dangerous effect of this kind of advertising is that humans gradually become accustomed to according reason and truth, rationality and credibility too little esteem.

In light of the fact (to be discussed in the next section of this book) that political propaganda also employs all of these perfected means and methods of advertising, Aldous Huxley asks, justifiably, if any prospect exists at all of arousing and appealing to the responsible rationality of humans, if the attempt to achieve a rationally oriented development of human society is not senseless. At the moment it appears as if human reason must founder on the overwhelming power exerted by an advertising technique that is not always managed in a morally accepted manner. That advertising controls the political process in the same way it controls the market economy is a special reason for being concerned.

Obviously this manipulation of information is harmful, and harmful in the highest degree. Intraspecific communication among animals that consists of mendacious propaganda has been proved to be counterproductive. A. Zahavi has demonstrated this convincingly. We can expect that in intrahuman communications, too, honesty and truthfulness will gradually prove themselves to be more advantageous, the best policy. I have lived a very long time and I am, despite everything, still optimistic. I even believe that I can detect a certain trend toward more honesty in the media.

COLLECTIVE-AGGRESSIVE ENTHUSIASM AND POLITICAL PROPAGANDA

"The task of the commercial propagandist in a democracy," says Aldous Huxley in *Brave New World Revisited,*

> is in some ways easier and is some ways more difficult than that of a political propagandist employed by an established dictator or a dictator in the making. It is easier in as much as almost everyone starts out with a prejudice in favour of beer, cigarettes and refrigerators, whereas almost nobody starts out with a prejudice in favour of tyrants. It is more difficult in as much as the commercial propagandist is not permitted, by the rules of his particular game, to appeal to the more savage instincts of his public. The advertiser of dairy products would dearly love to tell his readers and listeners that all their troubles are caused by the machina-tions of a gang of godless international margarine manufac-turers, and that it is their patriotic duty to march out and burn the oppressors' factories. This sort of thing, however, is ruled out, and he must be content with a milder approach.

Effective political propaganda profits from an originally species-preserving behavior norm of humans that can, how-ever, when appealed to among the mass societies of mod-ern civilization, become especially dangerous: the feeling of collective-aggressive enthusiasm. Originally this norm served in the defense of one's own group, the family. Almost every human male knows the subjective experience that accompanies the mode of behavior discussed here: a shudder runs along the spine and, as one can determine through closer observation, also over the outer sides of the arms. One cannot avoid perceiving the quality of this excitation as having a high value and the prickling of the skin as being a "sacred shudder." The German word *Begeisterung* already expresses the possession of a person by something higher, something essentially human, the human spirit (*Geist*) or soul. The English word "enthusiasm" — derived from the Greek word *enthousiasmos,* from *enthousiazein,* to be inspired, from *entheos,* inspired, a combination of *en-* plus *theos,* god — implies even more: that a god has seized hold and taken possession of a human.

One begins to doubt the godlike nature of this "sacred shudder" when one becomes acquainted with the behavior pattern, quite certainly homologous, of our nearest zoological relative, the chimpanzee. In my book *On Aggression,* I have described the objectively observable behavior that is associated with the experience of enthusiasm in the following way:

> The tone of the entire striated musculature is raised, the carriage is stiffened, the arms are raised from the sides and slightly rotated inward so that the elbows point outward. The head is proudly raised, the chin stuck out, and the facial muscles mime the "hero face," familiar from the films. On the back and along the outer surface of the arms the hair stands on end. This is the objectively observed aspect of the shiver!

This standing on end of the body hair permitted, in the relatively near past, the threatening posture of the male to appear a bit more frighteningly impressive. In any case, this movement norm must have originated during a time when humans had not yet stood as upright as they do today. When one is upright, bristling hairs on the back and on the nape are not visible to a hostile opponent one is facing; in the normal posture a chimpanzee assumes, the bristling of body hairs enlarges its contours in a most impressive way. There can be no doubt about the homology of the behavior pattern of the human and of the chimpanzee.

Like other instinctive programmed behavior patterns, those of collective-aggressive enthusiasm are also released by a combination of quite sharply definable stimulus situations. As among chimpanzees, the objects for whose defense we are ready to engage ourselves enthusiastically have a *social* nature.

Humans respond with virtually reflexive predictability to situations calling for combative defense of any kind of social unit. This unit can be quite concretely the family, the nation, the alma mater or the football team, or even an abstraction such as the work ethic of natural science research, the incorruptibility of artistic creation or the marvelousness of bygone fraternity days. Just as it is also true for other emotions, the reaction of enthusiasm is not at all inhibited by the insight that its object is not worth such an unreserved involvement.

As part of the overall stimulus situation in which collective-aggressive enthusiasm is released belongs, as an effective key stimulus, the presence of a threat to values that must be defended. The demagogue knows very well that such an image of the enemy can also fulfill its purpose when it has no factual basis, when the threat is pure fabrication. Moreover, the threat can be presented as something concrete or as something completely abstract — "the" nonbelievers, "the" Boches, "the" Huns, tyrants or "the Barbarians" are just as good for his purposes as "capitalism" or "communism" or "imperialism" or any of the other "isms."

The special danger of the psychophysiological condition such enthusiasm entails is that, in this temper of mind and for the humans involved, all values seem completely insignificant except the one for which they are, at the moment, so enthusiastic. While perceiving the subjective experience of enthusiasm as having an "uplifting" quality, one also feels, given these circumstances, exempt from all the values of everyday life; one is ready to let everything else take care of itself in order to obey the call of this "sacred duty."

Heinrich Heine has his hero say (and I think he intended no irony): "*Was shert mich Weib, was shert mich Kind, ich trage weit besseres Verlangen, laß sie betteln gehen, wenn sie hungrig sind. Der Kaiser, der Kaiser gefangen!*" [What's wife to me, what's child, by a far nobler need enraptured, let them go beg, if they are hungry. The emperor, the emperor captured!] When, in this condition of collective enthusiasm, the value one attaches to one's own family can be neglected, it is not at all astonishing that other norms of social behavior can also be pushed aside and ignored. What is most regrettable is that all instinctive inhibitions against injuring and killing one's fellow humans lose much of their power. Through a remarkable reversal of all value conceptions, rational considerations are often made to appear not only untenable but also base and dishonorable; criticisms of, and all reasonable arguments against, the behavior dictated by collective-aggressive enthusiasm are silenced. A Ukrainian proverb says: "When the flag is flying, all reason is in the trumpet."

This proverb can be translated into the terminology of brain physiology: when the midbrain speaks, it silences the neocortex. Demagogues have known this for a long time and, unfortunately with justification, count on their propaganda campaigns to silence completely among the masses they choose to influence each and every activity of the cerebrum. In *Mein Kampf* Hitler expressed himself with astonishing frankness when writing about his methods. He knew all the strategies of modern mass psychology for targetting propaganda; he calculated quite accurately the cumulative effect of being swept along, and he paid tribute to the suggestive efficacy of marching together and singing together. In *On Aggression* I wrote, "Singing along means giving the devil an inch."

When I wrote that book, I was of the opinion that war, an entire ethnic group becoming aggressive toward another ethnic group, was institutional and thus culture-dependent. When someone opposed my point of view on the basis of a misunderstanding and titled an article he wrote "War Is Not in Our Genes," my answer was: "But I never maintained that it was." In the meantime, unfortunately, observations made by Jane van Lawick-Goodall about chimpanzees living in the wild have confirmed among these creatures the occurrence of genuine warring expeditions. The "warmongers" involved in these operations show expressive gestures and movements that are exactly comparable to those described above for humans. The chimpanzees egg one another on into a reciprocally escalated state of "enthusiasm," that is, collective aggressivity; then, closing ranks, they attack a neighboring horde of chimpanzees, going first for the strongest male. In the case that was observed, the attackers killed all the individuals of the "enemy" band within a short time. Since one would hardly choose to ascribe cultural institutions to these anthropoid apes, one must conclude that the action and reaction norms of such a collective attack are, contrary to all expectations, genetically programmed after all.

Thus that much more necessary does it become to gird mankind, especially young people and the enthusiasm-prone of every age, against the dangers that accrue through their own reaction norms and through the calculated use made of these by every form of demagoguery. That the inborn, generally human capacity for becoming enthusiastic about particular values can be extremely dangerous does not also mean that this capacity is *dispensable*. As I pointed out in the section covering the perceptions of values, the entire apparatus for human ratiocination and human reasoning would be without every dynamic impetus were not instinctively programmed behavior norms functioning as the motor driving all of the machinery. Only in the rarest instances, only among the "borderline cases," are behavior programs completely "closed"; just as rare are "open programs" as defined by Ernst Mayr, that is, programs of behavior determined almost exclusively by a learning process. While every form of enthusiasm can be characterized as comprising the givens of subjective experience, expressive movements and the suppression or even active exclusion of perceptions of all other values, the object of the enthusiasm is determined extensively by what has been acquired. Thus, to the extent that the already mentioned key-stimulus situations have been set up, collective-aggressive enthusiasm can take as its object an abstract ideal or something as completely concrete as a soccer team.

We know another process determining the choice of an object by which a very complex behavior program that is otherwise extensively enclosed within itself is fixed onto an object, the process called imprinting. In most cases its function is the fixation of *social* behavior patterns onto their appropriate objects, in such cases onto conspecifics. A distinctive attribute of this kind of object imprinting is its irrevocability. It was just this attribute that guided the attention of researchers to the uniqueness of this process: animals of various species, reared by humans who, very early on in the lives of those animals, substituted themselves as the animals' parents, grew up incapacitated for breeding because all of their patterns of sexual behavior had been irreversibly fixated on humans as sexual partners. Adhering to the object fixations of enthusiasm are certain features similar to those associated with imprinting. I have already mentioned that there is a phase of individual development among humans, adolescence, during which young people are especially ready to accept new values as their own and just as ready to abandon the traditional values of their parents. This bonding process has certain similarities to the processes of imprinting. Yet the duration of the sensitive phase that can be presumed here is less sharply delimited and the choices of the objects that are made are not irrevocable. They are fortunate who, during this sensitive phase of their youth, can find ideals to advocate that are worthy of the complete commitment of humane human beings.

INDOCTRINATION

All the demagogues of every era were, and still are, aware of the fact that humans serve most faithfully those ideals they make their own while they are still young. Demagogues have always known, but they know even more now about how to concoct the key-stimuli artificially and how to present these most attractively.

One must have talked with young people who have really dedicated themselves to a doctrine before it is possible for one to have any idea about the total nonchalance with which early enthusiasts are deaf to all counterarguments and with which they can dismiss all other values. "What's wife to me, what's child . . ." is but a weak description of the entirety, the totality, of all those things enthusiasts no longer care about. Most remarkable in this connection is the fact that such a thorough submission to a doctrine apparently imparts to each indoctrinated person the most complete and consummately comforting feeling of personal freedom. The captive identifies completely with the ideals instilled in him by the doctrinaire; he does not even feel the straitjacket into which he has been strapped. The thoroughly indoctrinated person does not notice that he has been deprived of a constituent feature of true humanity, the freedom to think. The expression on the faces of those who are absolutely convinced is such that it incites rather more anger in everyone they deign to talk with than the commiseration every indoctrinated person actually deserves.

The corresponding syndrome of significant expressive movements — the facial expressions reflecting emotions, the gestures and the actions of the body, the vocal intonations — I was able to observe consciously for the first time in 1922, in America, at a New York university, in a fellow student who was, for a European, a "revivalist," that is, an adherent of a movement endeavoring to restore Christianity to active and dynamic life. At the time we met I had already read enough about the theory of evolution to be able to discuss the dogmas of Genesis with this young man. In the process I was introduced for the first time to the rigid inflexibility of indoctrination. This expression of indoctrinated enthusiasm is most clearly and unmistakably presented by many of the modern Russian and even some of the Chinese placards mounted on billboards.

My second introduction to the syndrome of indoctrinated

enthusiasm occurred during the time I spent as a prisoner of war in Russia, from 1944 until 1948, when I got to know it very well. There I experienced again something that brought back my acquaintance with the young revivalist in New York as a vivid memory: the genuine enthusiast for a doctrine regards it as his or her duty to make proselytes. Many of the younger military officers and medical doctors whom I got to know fairly well during my activities as a physician in the Soviet Union attempted to convert me. When one of these people began to be friendlier and, in relation to the prisoner I was, began to relax his quiet reserve, I could just about predict when the attempt at conversion would begin. It must also be said that, with the greatest consistency, these zealously missionizing Soviet citizens were basically decent and good people; in many cases I did not have the heart to explain why and how unacceptable their doctrine was to me.

One thing, however, became clear to me through these Soviet Russian missionizing attempts that had eluded me earlier during the conversion attempts made by the revivalist. It is the fact that those who are most socially oriented and inclined, who are good-hearted and decent, are especially defenseless against the machinations of indoctrinating demagogues. What hinders them most of all from freeing themselves from the doctrine, even when they have become fully aware of its worthlessness, is actually a real virtue — their fidelity. When one has grasped fully the tragedy of this fidelity, one can also realize the responsibility that exists to protect young people from the tar babies of indoctrination of every sort.

·•✦[NINE]✦•·

Errant Meanderings of the Human Mind

OVERVALUED IDEAS AND NEUROSES

In the preceding chapter behavior norms were discussed — norms genetically determined or traditionally established — that, in themselves, are completely meaningful and healthy and lead to failed performance only through the rapidly increasing mass of human beings, the enormous quantity of owned possessions and the prodigious amounts of readily available energy contributing to an environment with conditions that are no longer suitable for those norms. It is something essentially and completely different when human behavior itself becomes "crazy." The uncommonly prevalent neuroses in our current civilization, the false assessment of reality and the mistaken importance placed on many things result in humans, collectively as well as individually, striving for what is detrimental and damaging. Sharp distinctions naturally do not exist between the two phenomena.

Neurosis can quite well be defined as a process allowing

particular ideas gradually to become overvalued until they finally assume control of the entire personality of a person and force silence upon all other motivations. It would be a misconception to believe that I would like to explain all the disorders that are to be discussed here as repressed conflicts. I have defined the human mind as a *collective* phenomenon, as all of the knowledge, capabilities and aspirations held in common, conferred upon humanity through its capacities for conceptual thinking and for syntactical language. Under "mental illness" I understand, consequently, only morbidities of the collective mind of mankind; I call these *epidemic* neuroses.

Regrettably almost all the neuroses fitting the definition given above and rampant today in the Western world have in common that they suppress just those characteristics and capabilities that we esteem as constituting true *humanity*. A typical example of a neurosis by which the personality of a human is gradually "consumed" to the extent that he is no longer interested in anything else is greed for money. A behavior norm of desiring to own is naturally present normally; that this norm is founded on a genetic program is dubious. In our culture several positive reciprocal effects certainly exist between the motivations for competition and those for wanting to own; moreover, already acquired possessions appear to exert a positive reciprocal effect on the urge to acquire still more possessions. The pathological nature of the phenomenon being discussed expresses itself in the inexorable power it exerts over the afflicted person. He is driven to work harder than a slave owned by the most atrocious master.

The drive to get the better of one's fellow humans leads likewise to overvalued ideas under the pressure of which many civilized people can be found suffering today. The ambition to get ahead in one's career at all costs is a hallmark of our success-oriented society. Competition is revealed at its worst among humans wherever monetary aspects are a concern; "time is money" is a true but also a most deplorable declaration.

A third motivation interacting in unison with the drives that have become addictions, getting more money and winning all competitions, is the innate striving of humans for rank and social position that was discussed in the section on competition. All three motivations together join to form a vicious circle in which humanity is caught, is whirled around ever faster and faster, and out of which it becomes more and more difficult to step, to exit.

THEORETICAL AND ACTUAL EFFECTS OF SCIENTISM

In the second part of this book it was pointed out that scientism, or ontological reductionism, denies subjective experience any claim to being real; here, in the section concerned with the maladies of the collective human mind, it is essential to point out that, as Teilhard de Chardin accurately discerned, scientism lets the value difference extant between the more simple and the more complex living systems disappear completely. The damage done by this disappearance can be illustrated by a simple example. The assertion that "Life processes are chemical-physical processes" is completely correct. What else could they be — at least for the scientist who absolutely refuses to believe in miracles? In contrast to the assertion made above, a second assertion that "Life processes are actually nothing but chemical-physical processes" is patently false. Specifically what is essential for life processes (for their being what they are), what is theirs alone, differentiates them from other chemical-physical processes. The misleading results of ontological reductionism can be made still more evident when I place in comparison with one another two additional statements having an even greater span of value difference: "Man is a mammal within the order of primates" is just as apparently correct as the statement "Man is actually nothing but a mammal within the order of primates" is obviously false. For such errors Julian Huxley coined the wonderful designation "nothing-else-buttery."

No scientist may succumb to the folly of believing he is not dependent on the public opinion of his day. The dangerous spirit of the times, the threatening *Zeitgeist* controlling the world today, has been born out of a dislocation in the conscious awareness of what is real and afflicts a majority of the humans who are both Western and civilized. In their book about the social constructs of reality, Thomas Luckmann and Peter Berger have shown that a human can regard as important and, above all, as *real* only that which qualifies as important and real in the society in which he matures and with which, moreover, he himself has daily contact. Most civilized humans are now city-dwellers or, at least, have jobs in cities. Here I reemphasize that, in their daily lives, these people come in contact almost exclusively with only nonliving and, above all, with man-made things, and they have learned to come to terms with almost all of them. I also repeat that they have, however, unlearned how to get on with everything else that is alive; they treat everything living, wherever and whenever they make contact, with sheer, unbelievable shortsightedness, and proceed to destroy what is vital and animate sustaining every one of us. Because everything with which they have daily contact and what they regard as real has been made by humans, they regard everything as *makable;* that something alive, once destroyed, cannot be made alive again has perhaps never been consciously acknowledged by them, or this knowledge has been suppressed. The blatant misconception that absolutely everything is makable and doable and repairable is fortified by the colossal power that has accrued to mankind through knowledge growing out of the *exact* sciences. These sciences, in their turn, are based on analytical mathematics, and proofs of their accuracy can be demonstrated for all those who put no faith in them.

Now, in an actual and practical sense, these epistemologically mistaken paths of human thought and reasoning have irremediable consequences which, on their part, exert a "positive" reciprocal effect on the epidemic madness. The dislocation of reality suffered by modern urban humans, because they are in daily contact only with nonliving, inanimate, man-made objects, befalls, unfortunately, in its most acute form, humans in positions of power who should be bearing the responsibilities for mankind's weal and woe. Yet what is real for them, what they affect and what, reciprocally, affects them and what they think about continually is influence and *money*. Money can be quantified with extraordinary ease; one can count on money and calculate with it; currencies allow themselves to be manipulated. No wonder, then, that ecologists are regarded as "nostalgic dreamers" when they warn that cash in paper or metal, even in gold itself, or numbers in a bankbook or on a balance sheet are mere symbols and that the real necessities of life, such as pure air and unpoisoned water and uncontaminated soil and an intact protective ozone layer above the earth's surface, will very soon no longer be buyable for all the money in the world.

Even more than the other epidemic neuroses and lunacies of our present day, the dislocations of perceived reality currently gripping the world economy have assumed an influence on scientific thinking. Every scientist, be he among the greatest, is a child of his time and must be this — otherwise he would not be understood at all. However this may be, it will be an extraordinarily difficult task for the natural sciences to oppose and replace as predominant the insidious influence of ontological reductionism.

·⊰[PART FOUR]⊱·

The Present Position
of Mankind

·∘][TEN][∘·

The Technocratic System

OPTIMISM ON PRINCIPLE

The position into which mankind has maneuvered itself through its intellectual capacities is, summarily stated, desperate. Despite this judgment, I do not share Oswald Spengler's outlook that the fate of our culture is sealed. Quite the contrary; everyone who has read Karl Popper can be convinced that every attempt to predict the future is logically impossible. The system of human societal organization, the maladies of which we have been concerned with in this book, is quite unequivocally the most complicated system extant on our planet. I have tried hard in this book to organize the sequence of the sections in such a way that the symptoms of illness would be intelligible and understandable as having been engendered by the failed performances of the human mind that were discussed in the second part of this book. When I designate the currently dominant societal order as the "technocratic system," this is done because technology threatens to establish itself as a tyrant over mankind. An activity that by its nature should be a means to an end has become an end in itself. When something becomes technically possible now, it is regarded as a duty, as an obligation, to *realize* this possibility. The branches of science underlying and supporting technology directly have become overvalued while the significance of all other branches of science has become undervalued. The scientism discussed in chapter 3, and all its dangerous effects, stands in direct causal interaction with technocracy.

The complication of the technocratic system makes precise insight into the details of its structural web of effects basically impossible. For this reason we must be aware, from the very beginning, that the human mind has here created a system involving such complications that the mind's own complexity is inadequate for comprehending it completely. Nevertheless it is meaningful to undertake a presentation of the discernible *disturbances* that threaten the continued functioning of the system. Even without complete insight into the disturbed system, one can recognize the causes of the disturbances and seize upon meaningful countermeasures. Even without penetrating insight into the dominant societal order, the impression is beginning to gain ascendancy among young people that the continued explosive growth of the earth's population and of the world's economy can lead only to catastrophe, and that the progressional division of labor and overorganization threatens to lead to a spiritual impoverishment of mankind and to the loss of essential inherent human rights.

STABILIZING MECHANISMS OF THE SYSTEM

The predominant system has set in motion processes of economic and technical development that can be reversed only with difficulty or not at all, and the prolongation of which menace mankind, as a species, with destruction. To these dangers I devoted an entire book, *Civilized Man's Eight Deadly Sins*. Here I am concerned with other dangers, certainly closely connected with those treated in the earlier book, yet related not to the demise of humankind but pertinent to the waning of mankind's humaneness. There exists, absolutely, the possibility that the human race will elude extinction despite poisoned air and water, overpopulation, radioactivity, and a depleted ozone layer; while the race somehow may survive these very real dangers, there also exists the second possibility that a rigid state-controlled sociopolitical organization of humanity will, at the same time and as a consequence, come to prevail and force mankind's subsequent development further away from the humane in an uninterrupted descending trajectory.

Commercial enterprises achieve that much more stability the larger they become. It is altogether conceivable that large multinational enterprises, combining within all of the countries concerned, could consolidate themselves into a world-domineering power. If this were to happen, the open society on which the continuity of our humaneness depends, would be destroyed, as Karl Popper has convincingly shown. A closed society is by definition *nonhuman*. In his books *Brave New World* and *Brave New World Revisited*, Aldous Huxley described a ghastly vision of a future culture: in this world a strict organization confines immense masses of people within forced work groups tyrannically determined and controlled to the most minute details — an organization based on the tremendous treasure of all-inclusive human "scientific" information, but purposely allowing the single individual access to only a minimal part of this total knowledge. Nevertheless, each individual human believes himself to be happy and satisfied since, from the cradle onward, he has been subjected to tried-and-true indoctrination, and this feeling of well-being is sustained through the use of psychopharmaceuticals. Such an apparatus of sovereign authority as that so frighteningly depicted by Aldous Huxley always develops, through an extended existence, mechanisms committed to the suppression of every heresy. All human reactions of fidelity, loyalty and enthusiasm are calculatedly motivated and canalized so that dissidents can be branded as dumb, bad, and traitorous, or can be declared out of their minds. The more extensive such a system becomes and the larger the population mass is that believes in the system's dogmatic statutes, that much greater will be its suggestive effectiveness and that much more effective will be the phenomena (here being discussed) that appear as a result of "self-immunization" — as T. Kuhn labeled them. It is an alarming fact that the phenomena of self-immunization can already be remarked, as well, in those areas concerned with the formation of scientific opinion. Apparently this is a result, in the sciences, of a "loss of individuality and the leveling of social and intellectual characteristics to mass accommodation." There are now too many scientists who choose not to acknowledge new ways of thinking. The self-immunization could lead to a complete drying up of natural science knowledge.

One can, in a somewhat macabre way, describe it as a piece of good luck that humans, with their current average genetic inclinations, would not be able to tolerate regimentation into a technocratic social ordering. I concur with Erich Fromm's opinion that, under the pressures placed on one's life by today's civilization, only a person with completely wrongheaded inclinations can escape serious psychic disturbances.

The enormous mass of humans alive today provides a certain restraint against rapid genetic modifications, but it cannot be predicted how long the gene pool of present-day mankind, however massive its numbers may be, can resist a *selection pressure* that, in a *most incisive way, favors* the readiness for uncritical *subordination and* the capacity for being open to *indoctrination.* When contemplating this possibility it should be remembered that humans themselves, and within a relatively short span of historical time, were able to breed out of their domestic animals, as good as completely, all drives for independence and for freedom of movement.

THE CESSATION OF SELECTION

The creative factors of evolution, above all free mutation and selection, brought the human mind into being. Then, however, the human mind cut out the effective force of selection in that it contrived to suspend almost all hostile impingements originating from its external world — predacious animals, debilitating climate, infectious diseases and the like. Now the human stands upright at the peak of creation: "Stand or fall!" The unsteadiness of his upright stance can, in truth, be taken as symbolic for the uncertainty of his position.

As I attempted to show in chapter 5, many of the innate as well as traditional norms of humans that were still well-adapted programs of social and economic behavior just a short while ago today contribute to the waning of what is humane. As I have already stated, cultural change now proceeds at such a rapid pace that there is no hope whatsoever in anticipating a phylogenetic adaptation to these new circumstances.

But the creative function of selection has not only been abolished; it has been turned into its own antithesis. The aspects of selection that still remain effective today are headed in the direction of depravity. The hope that a *cultural* development could counteract genetic "Sacculinisation" (see chapter 2) appears small. There are good reasons for the assumption that a culturally higher development differs in no essential way from the phyletic in that, in the game of universal interaction, apparently all "upwardly" oriented creative development depends upon its being carried out among *variegated* cultures.

The technocratic system dominating the world today is at the point of leveling off all cultural differences. All of the peoples on the earth, with the exception of those described as underdeveloped, produce the same articles by means of the same techniques, plow with the same tractors fields that are planted with the same monocultures, and go to war with the same weapons. But above all they compete within the same world market and do their best, using the same methods of propaganda, to outdo one another. More and more, the qualitative differences that could be creatively effective in this interplay are disappearing. B.-O. Küppers has shown that a decline of cultural values corresponds to a disappearance of natural diversity.

It is a pernicious error on the part of the science of economics to suppose that the "natural selection" of a free market economy might be regarded with as much certainty as a creative beneficent force as that of natural selection in the evolution of species. The criteria for selection in economic life are those associated exclusively with rapid power acquisition. According to Küppers, the value concept of economics has a pronounced normative character and thus loses automatically its temporal universality. As I attempted to show in the section on cultural evolution in chapter 3, excessive conservatism begets "living fossils," while at the other extreme all too excessive variableness produces monsters incapable of surviving. This is so in the development of cultures just as it is in the evolution of species.

A much too rapid development in a culture dominated by technology carries with it, as characteristic, the penchant for that culture to strike out often in shortsighted directions from which there is no turning aside or turning back. Many processes in our technical civilization are like control system circuits with positive feedback that, once set in motion, are difficult to stop. Economic growth and the growing needs felt by consumers, implanted through propaganda, are an example of this. But the crassest example of all is the utilization of nuclear energy: a nuclear power plant has a use-life of, at the most, between twenty and thirty years — simply because of the normal and known factors of construction deterioration — but the plants themselves remain unalterably radioactive for about 20,000 years — the half-life of the accumulated nuclear waste. Since every nuclear power plant wants to and must sell the energy it produces, its existence induces the establishment of a commensurate industry that, after the said twenty to thirty years, makes the construction of another new nuclear power plant necessary. Dangers of this sort arising from irreversible developments are never mentioned by those who are responsible for them; through shortsighted and irresponsible decisions made by humans, economic-technical programs are firmly established that are not only ecologically naive but are blind to the values inherent in living nature. But a majority of the humans alive today can manage only passive resistance to such a phylogenetically downward development (in the sense described in chapter 2).

The only legitimate energy "intake source" of our planet is solar, and every sustained economic growth that uses more energy than the sun sends us puts the world economy in debt, and in debt to a completely callous and uncompromising creditor. The so-called Meadows Report by the Massachusetts Institute of Technology tells us the very same thing; nevertheless, at a *Tagung der Energiewirtschaft* held in Vienna not long ago, it was maintained that those people who oppose the use of atomic energy are moved to protest "primarily for *emotional* reasons." Faced with this interpretation and description, I confess to feeling emotion, too.

THE PSEUDODEMOCRATIC DOCTRINE

Among the factors stabilizing the technocratic system belongs the doctrine of the absolute equality of all humans, in other words, the erroneous belief that the human is born as a *tabula rasa,* a blank tablet, a clean slate, and that his entire personal identity and personality are determined, initially, by learning processes. This doctrine in which, unfortunately, many people still believe even today with nothing less than religious fervor, had its origin, as Philip Wylie shows us in his book *The Magic Animal,* in a misrepresentation of a famous phrase found in the American Declaration of Independence drafted by Thomas Jefferson. There it states "that all men are created equal." These words were written at a time when the British colonies in America, "being as yet perfectly independent of each other," chose to unite and declare themselves independent of Great Britain in order to achieve "among the powers of the earth the separate and equal station" they were entitled to. The fundamental act of union was based, ultimately, on the rights of man, on the free right to the unbounded exercise of reason and freedom of opinion. As Jefferson explained in one of the last letters he wrote: "the mass of mankind has not been born with saddles on their backs, nor a favored few booted and spurred, ready to ride them legitimately, by the grace of God." As effective as the declaration was, so also was the subsequent double distortion of the phrase's logic: the first incorrect deduction was that if all humans had ideal conditions for development, they would develop into ideal beings. From this incorrect deduction it was further inferred, in another logical somersault, that all humans at birth are absolutely identical. J. B. Watson, as is known, went so far as to claim that, out of every healthy newly born child left in his care for rearing, he could make "to order" a violin virtuoso, a mathematician or a financial genius. The false assumption being made here is that there are no genetically fixed programs whatsoever in the central nervous system of humans, and that all of the individual differences of human behavior are to be explained through differences in individual experience, as conditioned. Just this is what the "empty organism" theory of B. F. Skinner maintains.

The assumption that apart from whatever can be inculcated in him through "conditioning" a human possesses no natural norms of any sort of social behavior has the automatic consequence that the blame for every misbehavior and every criminal action can be laid on the rearing of the delinquent. The individual human is, in this manner and by these means, absolved from all moral responsibility; that, at the same time, he is also robbed of one of his rights as a human, namely the right of responsibility, is more often than not ignored completely.

The belief in the unlimited plasticity of humans is naturally most welcome to all those people for whom it would be advantageous if the human possessed no inborn abilities and capacities and would, thus, be unlimitedly manipulatable. This explains why the pseudodemocratic doctrine that all men are equal, by which is believed that all humans are initially alike and pliable, could be made into a state religion by both the lobbyists for large industry and by the ideologues of communism. The pseudodemocratic doctrine continues to exert tremendous influence on public opinion and on psychology. That this is so is most certainly related to population numbers and to the overorganization of civilized humanity these numbers have necessitated, within which allowances for individual differences can no longer be made with any sufficiency. One runs counter to claims for "equal opportunities" if one says a person is intelligent or dumb or dishonest, although everyone knows that there are dumb people and intelligent people as well as those who are honest and others who are dishonest. Actually making the indisputable assertion that, with the exception of single-egg twins, there are no two humans with completely identical genetical programming can, as Philip Wylie correctly confirmed, be just as dangerous today, in some parts of the world, as it was in the Middle Ages to maintain that the earth circled the sun and not the other way round.

HOSPITALISM AS AN EXAMPLE

Humans thinking scientistically and technomorphically have, as has been emphasized, forgotten how to cope with everything else that is also living. Several decades ago this was true as well for the ways in which humans behaved toward their own offspring. If one believes that all aspects of feeling are illusionary, if one strives toward a soulless psychology, then, consequently, one can also not sense any sympathy for a human baby, left alone in the darkness of a bedroom, who continues to cry despairingly for help. There have been times when it was regarded as enlightened to let children simply scream, and also not to feed them according to their arising needs, on demand, but according to a clocked schedule. Above all, that infants must accustom themselves to sleeping alone in a room was promoted to nothing less than a dogma. All young animals of every diurnal species still dependent on parental care are fated for virtually certain death if, in pitch-darkness, they become separated from their families. Teleonomically it is a completely meaningful program that prompts the baby, be it a gosling or a human infant, in such a situation to use the entire supply of nervous and muscular energy it has available in sending out cries for help.

Much graver and more ominous are the consequences that technomorphic thinking had for the "enlightened" and "rational" treatment of infants in the nurseries of children's homes and hospitals. For a long time in those institutions the opinion prevailed that all the needs of their babies would be met if they were fed regularly with the prescribed amount of food, were given vitamins as well, and were kept sufficiently clean. What was being neglected because it was not yet known about at the time is a very firmly fixed, programmed phase in the individual development of human social behavior: between the fifth and the eighth month of life, the infant's capacity for differentiating among individual people develops and, at the same time, the bonding to a particular individual begins; under normal circumstances, the bonding naturally is to the mother. With the wisdom of age, old women in Austria say *"das Kind beginnt zu fremdeln"* [the infant has begun to distinguish strangers]. The smile that, until recently, could have been elicited by everyone who bent over the infant's bed, also smiling and appearing friendly, from now on is given only to a quite particular reference person.

The development of that smile and the key stimuli that release it were studied in detail by René Spitz. To him goes the credit for being the first to examine the nature of the innate releasing mechanism and for having comprehended what came to be known as the law of heterogeneous summation — although a comprehensive conceptualization of this law remained stalled initially between the lines of description. Even the very young infant smiles when an air-filled balloon on which dots for eyes and dashes for eyebrows have been painted is held above its crib and made to nod; the infant's smile reaction is stronger when a friendly grinning mouth is added to the balloon's eyes and eyebrows. At first René Spitz could not understand why his own smiling and nodding over a crib were less effective in releasing a response than were these same actions performed by his dark-haired female assistant. When he saw himself reflected in a mirror, and at an angle comparable to that from which he would be seen by the child, he recognized that the nodding of his assistant provided color changes between pink and brownish-black, while his own movements, because of his baldness, gave an impression of unchanging pink. After he had put on a dark stocking cap the differences between the releasing effects disappeared.

Only a few weeks later crude models can no longer release the smile, although all normal human heads still can, especially when they nod and smile. At the time of "distinguishing friends from strangers," the reaction becomes even more selective, to the extent of becoming limited to a particular individual. The period that now follows is extremely critical for the child's entire further development: the infant now begins to bond its feelings to a specified person. All other humans are rejected. When this critical period is reached in a home for children or in a hospital and the baby has begun to bond itself to a particular nurse, as it would to its mother, routinely instigated personnel changes destroy this budding relationship. The unfortunate infant now tries, with reactions already substantially less resolute, to attach itself to the next substitute mother; when this one is also torn away, with an even weaker effort to the next, until finally all attempts to establish a mother-bonding are given up entirely. From now on the baby fends off all stimuli coming from members of its species, turns its face to the wall, and some of these children end up autistic or they simply die.

This bonding to a specific, individual mother figure fosters the general capacity for forming all other later social bondings with one's fellow humans. The capacity for loving one's fellow humans is one of those apparently quite numerous nerve organizations of humans that, as they mature, must be claimed and responded to *at once* if they are not to suffer from atrophied activity or, in extreme cases, totally irretrievable inactivity.

Such a circumstance is, however, extremely dangerous because the personal friendship one has with someone particular, and the feelings of friendship one has for one's fellow humans in general, restrain aggressive behavior. As early on the evolutionary scale as the higher fishes it can be demonstrated that personal acquaintance impedes aggressivity.

A study should be made among violent criminals evidencing an obviously insufficient suppression of aggressivity, as demonstrated by terrorists, for example, on the way in which their social development progressed during very early childhood, especially at the time when "strangers" began to be distinguished. A hypothesis, not without foundation, that propounds an overall promotion of aggressivity, that is, a reduction of restraint to do evil to one's fellow humans, can be most closely connected with the impedance of the development of interhuman relationships during critical periods of earliest childhood.

Closely linked with the development of the capacity to love and to form friendships is, remarkably, the capacity for explorative behavior, for *curiosity,* as the Austrian child psychologist G. Czerwenka-Wenkstetten was able to determine. The empty, flabby faces of the young people who have been injured early on through total emotional deprivation show the unmistakable "pathophysiognomic" symptoms of this condition that, apparently, is difficult to heal or cannot be healed at all. Whoever is without any curiosity about anything is unavoidably, inevitably bored.

If my assumption is correct, then even low-grade hospitalism is one of the essential factors contributing to the "sensibility depletion" characteristic of our modern world.

THE DISLOCATION OF REALITY CONSCIOUSNESS

Tightly interwoven with technomorphic thinking and, like this way of thinking, one of the stabilizing supports of the technocratic system, is a dislocation, a displacement, of consciously acknowledged reality. As I have already mentioned, Peter Berger and Thomas Luckmann have shown that every human, of necessity, regards as real that with which he has most frequent contact, with whatever he usually interacts, and what he has most often on his mind. Remarkably late, only during the most recent past, has the number of natural scientists increased who, with a clinical eye, have recognized the dangers that threaten the living system of our planet. I recall, with considerable shame, having heard a lecture given by William Vogt about twenty years ago and not being in the least convinced that anything he said could justify the warnings he was giving us. The social behavior patterns of certain birds were more real to me at the time than were jeopardies to the human environment. Every human who is dedicated to his vocation, especially those who strive toward accomplishing self-set goals, holds the aspects of that vocation to be the most real and, moreover, the most important in the world. The industrialist who has fought with self-sacrificing devotion and real idealism for the formation and development of his firm perceives these endeavors to be, quite obviously, the only "interesting thing," the only real thing. All of the failed performances of human inclinations, all of the misapplications of natural propensities such as a love of order, the pleasure derived from witnessing increase, the joy of functioning and the others mentioned in chapter 5, can only confirm the industrialist in his conviction. Reinforcing all of these are, in addition, the scientistic and behavioristic world views: "correct" and "true" for the industrialist is what can be verified through quantification, and the making of money fulfills all of these numerical demands optimally.

All of these factors combined contrive to cause humans in organizations concerned with finance and with production to see the highest worth in our world concentrated in a production apparatus running smoothly at the highest possible speed making sustained maximal profits.

The pleasure derived from functioning, which has been discussed, can then take effect and result in the means soaring aloft to become the end in itself. When this happens, all of the humans involved become slaves to the apparatus of production. The vicious cycle of economic growth is then closed and subsequently becomes a maelstrom into which all mankind is sucked.

Those who represent the industries now dominating our globe, with all their available intelligence, appear to believe firmly in the reality of their subjective values. At the same time, however, they appear to be blind to two indisputable facts that every schoolchild is capable of comprehending:

first, that unlimited growth within a finite space cannot possibly go on forever; and second, that no properly budgeted household can give out more than it takes in. Those people who are responsible for our contemporary social order are quite certainly in a position to understand these facts; they are also not so immoral that they would be ready to expose their own children and grandchildren to a heinous extinction; they do not *believe* in the reality of the dangers that are threatening all of mankind because, for them, other things are real and consequently important.

The paradox to be found in these convictions quite commonly held lies in an apparent oversight on the part of so many people, regardless of their social status, that, as I have already pointed out, money and gold itself are merely symbols and that even with a great deal of money one cannot buy what is no longer there. That we can eat only what green plants manufacture by means of photosynthesis is something some humans seem not to want to believe. Two Austrian sayings express exactly what much of the world chooses to ignore: *"Goldene Nockerln kann mann nicht essen"* [Gold dumplings cannot be eaten] and *"Wo nichts ist, hat der Kaiser sein Recht verloren"* [Where nothing is, even an emperor has nothing to rule]. But the cup of the grotesque is brought to the brim when just those who emphasize the monetary to the exclusion of almost all else can consider themselves to be sober realists, can assume themselves to be good economists and at the same time regard ecologically oriented environmentalists as "nostalgic dreamers."

THE UNWANTED "AUTONOMOUS" HUMAN

The requirements of a technocratic system cannot accommodate normally inclined human beings, and the needs of normally inclined human beings cannot adequately be met within a technocratic system. There exist inborn behavior systems that are equivalent to human rights whose suppression can lead to serious mental disturbances. A technocratic system whose mode of formation and established structure I have attempted to present here in a roughly approximated and simplified form, can, of necessity, regard certain constitutive characteristics and accomplishments of humans as being not merely unnecessary but extremely troublesome. Any bonding of an individual human to another human in friendship, for example, is suppressed at every opportunity in totalitarian educational systems; at least the love one could come to have for a friend may not exceed the love one has for the system.

A waning of much that is essentially humane, the theme of this book, is not limited only to what is occurring within totalitarian systems; it is much more an inevitability that social constructs comprising vast numbers of people take on, once they have gone beyond certain limits, more and more totalitarian aspects, even when the social constructs choose to have themselves described as democracies. The laws governing this process are those of technocracy and not those of political ideology. In democracies, just as in dictatorships, the exercise of power over greater and greater numbers of humans becomes consolidated in the hands of an ever-decreasing number of humans occupying positions of power. I made this point earlier and need to state it again. It has been estimated that the number of aristocrats in whose hands the power of czarist Russia was concentrated would be about equal to the number of the successful lobbyists in present-day America, and would certainly also just about correspond to the number of so-called *Nomenklatura* in Russia today. This number has been given as two to four percent of the subject citizens.

Independent of the ideologies they profess, all current governing systems incorporate the tendency to abrogate the personality of the individual human being. Independent thinking and decision making on the part of the individual human is that much less desired the larger the national state structure becomes. One knows that small political units provide better opportunities for real democracy than do the very large nation-states. The greater the mass of humans is who adhere to a certain ideology, that much greater will be its suggestibility and that much more power will the doctrine in question accumulate. The greater the population to be governed becomes, that much more restrictive, of necessity, will the overorganized administration be, and that much further from the democratic ideal will the state structure have removed itself. Aldous Huxley has stated precisely that the freedom of the individual human being stands in an inverse ratio to the size of the nation-state of which he is a subject citizen.

The devaluations of individuality that occur within all large state structures avowing the most varied political convictions and, consequently, carried out in very different ways are, in their essence, extraordinarily similar.

The autonomous human being who stands on his rights to individuality and on his human rights is not the kind of citizen that is liked in large nation-states and, it should be noted, is not liked either by those doing the governing or by a majority of his fellow citizens being governed. The public opinion formed by this majority prescribes very exactly what "one" does or does not do; whoever behaves differently is, at the very least, suspect, or is regarded as not normal.

TAMING AND TRAINING METHODS

As outlined above, the convincing capacity of every doctrine increases with the number of humans controlled by it and, for that reason, the stability of the social order associated with the doctrine also, unfortunately, increases with the number of its subjects. But those who have the power in the large nation-states are not content to leave it at that; instead, they apply themselves assiduously to the utilization of various techniques for taming and training. The tried and true methods of conditioning are those of punishment or reward. Political systems openly professing their totalitarian character do not shy away from responding to all undesired behavior by meting out severe punishments. The population lives in constant anxiety but can, at the same time — and remarkably, for that is the way humans are made — feel genuine enthusiasm for its tyrants. In his book *Animal Farm,* George Orwell has sketched an apt and awful caricature of a totalitarian terror regime. The means he uses, the ways in which he shows how a majority of humans submit to such a regime only out of fear, and that only those who are the most naive can credulously be enthusiastic about its ideals, are just as unsettling as they are convincing. Orwell's presentation fits the fascistic state organization as well as sovietization. Still, in the Soviet Union, as in other large nation-states, taming and training through rewards is gradually being favored more and more. In China an analogous process appears to be taking place. Essentially what differentiates the taming-training methods that use punishments from those that use rewards are the contrasting sorts of opposition each of them evokes. Reigning with the whip generates an opposition that is downright heroic. A capitalistic domination of the masses through a provision of rewards, by means of a gradual coddling involving the cultivation of luxurious habits and expensive tastes, calls forth no heroes.

Thinking and philosophizing philanthropists recognized early the kinds of dehumanizing (in the most literal sense) consequences taming and training through pampering would bring in their wake. Decades ago Vance Packard showed convincingly in his book *The Hidden Persuaders* that, more than anything else, it is ease and convenience, the comfort of the individual, that prompts him to buy the products marketed by the big manufacturers. Each one of these new articles makes life a little bit more comfortable than the previous product was able to do. We are also certainly living during a period of "auto-cracy," that is, under the tyranny of the automobile. An entire series of the phenomena already discussed, much that has become so dangerous for our present generation, can be demonstrated using this locomotory prosthesis as the exemplification: joy of functioning, striving for a higher position in the rank order, interchanging the means and the end. Automobile manufacturers seduce the consumer with ever-increasing "driving comfort": the joy one has in driving seduces one to keep buying the newer models as they come on line. If one were to suggest to an older member of the middle class that he trade his present car for the model he had before, or the model he had before that one, he would become painfully aware that the suggestion involved a lowering of his standards *von Seide auf Stroh* [from silk (sheets) onto a straw (mattress)], and it would be pointed out to him how quickly he has accustomed himself to disk brakes and power steering and how thoroughly he has forgotten about the long-gone days of double-clutching — in other words, how well the manufacturers have succeeded in making him dependent on each of the new technical attainments. Moreover, I know of not a single case in which the latest model of a particular type and make of automobile was slower or had less horsepower than the model that preceded it.

Becoming accustomed to silk after straw is accomplished many times faster than is reaccustoming oneself to straw after silk. Today we are rarely aware, if we can remember at all, how uncomfortable life was for our parents, grandparents and great-grandparents at the turn of the century. I have lived long enough to remember exactly the many kerosene lamps that had to be cleaned and refilled and the many stoves that had to be loaded and lighted and tended daily in the houses of well-to-do burghers. If, today, any of us were to occupy rooms with the heating, lighting and washing facilities that seemed thoroughly acceptable to Privy Councillor von Goethe or to Duchess Anna Amalia von Weimar, or to their contemporaries John and Abigail Adams, we would regard ourselves as truly frugal — even if other people were to do all of the work for us.

Since ancient times it has been known that danger comes to hover near any human whenever "things are going too well," when any one of us is too successful in our natural endeavors to obtain ease and pleasure while avoiding discomfort. All of us have learned all too well how to steer clear of emphatically displeasurable situations; technology and pharmacology help us in this. We civilized humans are becoming continually less capable of supporting pain and sorrow. The extent of our fear of discomfort and the mechanics we set in motion to avoid it border on vice.

In *Civilized Man's Eight Deadly Sins,* I discussed the consequences this exaggerated avoidance of all unpleasurable experience has for obtaining pleasure and achieving joy. The old maxim from Goethe's poem *Schatzgräber* [Treasure-seeker], "*Saure Wochen, frohe Feste*" [Sour weeks, merry feast days], tells us that true joy is rendered unattainable through a sniveling insistence on an avoidance of all unpleasurable experience. At the most "pleasure" might still possibly be achieved without an honest price of unpleasure, in the form of "sour" (hard) work being made in payment, but not joy, not the *Freude schöner Götterfunken* that seems to set off beautiful, divine sparks. The increasing intolerance of the unpleasurable on the part of civilized humans transforms the naturally inevitable highs and lows of our normal lives into an artificially flattened expanse of monotonous gray, without any of the contrasts of lights and shadows. In short, this produces boredom and in so doing becomes the cause for so many humans needing to be continually entertained.

A need to be "entertained" is a symptom of an extraordinarily pitiable state of the human soul about which I am able to generalize from my own experience. I feel a need to read detective stories or to turn on the television set only when I am so tired, or when I have been so put out of action by something other than fatigue, that I am no longer capable of doing anything more demanding. Passively permitting oneself to be entertained is the exact opposite of creative activity; playing, by way of contrast, is the quintessence of that creative activity without which a truly humane world cannot continue to exist.

···❦[ELEVEN]❧···

The Present Position of Young People

Many of the processes discussed in Part Three, especially those in chapter 8, by means of which the developments undertaken by the human mind crowd in to vex and harass the human soul, are quite expressly disposed toward making life difficult for young people. Difficulties in accepting and then taking over parental tradition, the accumulation of social pressures and associated stresses, the restrictive over-organization and the forced specialization made necessary by a division of labor and career categorization — all these work together to reduce the joy young people have in being alive.

THE CRITICAL POINT

As I explained in Part One (particularly in chapter 3), the programming of human social ontogenesis is provided with certain mechanisms that, under the conditions of cultural development prevalent until recently, found the vitally necessary middle way between the firm retention of acquired structures and their dismantling and their restructuring.

Near the beginning of this book I cited Rabbi Ben Akiba's aphorism "Everything has been before." Whenever I give my sermon of warning for today's young people that sounds an alarm about the loss of tradition, I am very often presented with the rejoinder that older people have never been in agreement with younger people and that no culture has, as yet, disintegrated because of the conflict occurring between two succeeding generations. I have already emphasized that what happens in our world *never* repeats itself. The principle "Nothing has ever been before" applies to the present position of mankind exactly as it applies to all the stages of evolutionary development and to all that has happened in history.

Commensurate with the rapidity of cultural development, the stride taken by a generation to separate itself from the one that went before has, over time, lengthened. In order to be able correctly to transmit a tradition from one generation to the next, it is necessary for the younger generation to be able to identify with the older generation. This identification is dependent primarily upon the potency of the personal bondings that exist between the members of the younger and the older generations, but secondarily upon the extent of change that the culture in question has undergone during the course of one generation. This close contact, this love between members of two generations, is diminishing. Unfortunately we can see good reasons for this regrettable process.

The various national cultures have, for the most part, lost their singularities. In dress, in manners, and as far as most other customs are concerned, the peoples of all parts of the earth have gradually become more like one another. But at the same time the cultural distance between the generations in all cultures of the world has increased enormously. In our time we have reached a critical point: the young people of the most diverse nations and populations are more like one another than any of them are like their parents. The young people of every era have always, in the ways already described (chapter 3), revolted against the older generation, but nowadays one has the impression that the very dangerous critical point has been reached where members of the younger generation stand facing the older generation as if confronting a hostile and foreign ethnic group.

NATIONAL HATE

Erik Erikson's concept of cultural pseudo-speciation has already been mentioned. Also already stated is that cohesion of a group is effected, among other ways, through the commonly shared high estimation of group-specific behavior norms. That would all be well and good if it did not have to be paid for at a price that includes contempt, yes, even hatred, toward a comparable, rival group. We must directly confront the fact that between the generations worldwide today an emotional relationship has come to exist that thoroughly resembles the relationship existing between two neighboring tribes of Papuans or between two adjacent tribes of South American Indians. (Indians and Papuans decorate themselves with tribal specific body paint and pendants; the young people of today do something analogous and, in fact, in an astonishingly uniform manner.) In other words, children treat their parents as if they were members of an alien ethnic group.

Consciously setting oneself apart from another group is, among the other factors involved, also motivated by aggressivity — something that was made clear to me through self-observation. At the Institute for Comparative Behavioral Physiology at Seewiesen in Bavaria, Germany, a weekly colloquium was held that was marked by a truly wonderful lack of formality. In the circle of discussants were a lot of young people with long hair and beards, sometimes barefooted, dressed in blue jeans. One day I emerged from a reverie while dressing for the colloquium to find myself clothed in a suit, a white shirt and a tie. Suddenly it became clear to me that by doing this I would, for my part, be putting on the modern equivalent of war paint, and, ashamed, I actually changed clothes, putting on what I usually wore every day. A. Festetics also draws attention to the aggressive character of group-specific clothing.* As he reports, Hungarian as well as Slovakian national costumes are preserved in their purest forms where an enclave of one or the other of these groups has become isolated.

THE SENSITIVE PHASE FOR GROUP SELECTION

As was described in chapters 3 and 6, young people are especially open and responsive to every sort of propaganda just when they are at the stage of detaching themselves from the traditions of their families. At this time in their lives young people possess not only the capacity for becoming attached to a new group, they have an enormous need to do this. When young people in need of such an affiliation find no suitable group, they form one of their own, or even two, with the unrationalized goal of being able to enter the lists militantly for one's own group and against another group or, possibly, in appropriate instances against the entire world. The musical *West Side Story* presents a completely accurate picture of this process.

Kulturethologische und ökologische Aspekte pannonischer Volkstrachten [Culture-ethological and ecological aspects of Pannonian national dress]. In preparation.

It is self-evident that during this critical stage young people are exceedingly susceptible to propaganda of every kind; they have entered the open season for hunting and are sitting ducks for demagogues.

THE DRAINING AWAY OF MEANING

Young people who can think independently and who have quite accurately comprehended that the competitive striving for success of their parents' generation and that generation's one-sided belief in economic growth and rising Dow Jones industrial averages lead only into dead-end streets, can all too easily come to despair about the world as it is. Above all, if young people grow up in cities, in materialistic environments where interests are primarily financial and industrial, it is not surprising when they see in their successful and comfortably situated fathers no exemplary models worthy of imitation, especially when they also notice that such successful men are on the verge of heart attacks, are under constant stress and are not really happy at all. How accurate their insights are is verified by the results of many studies done on stress.

Just as little astonishment should be elicited when it is also discovered that young people are not terribly enthusiastic about democracy and its institutions, those political principles and policies to which their parents' generation have proclaimed their faith or at least have given lip service. Where should young people find and take their ideals? It still remains a kind of good fortune when they do not attach themselves to false ideals, such as those of the pseudoreligions, or simply escape from it all into drug addiction. It is also not very much better when, as the Roman *plebs* did for *panem et circenses*, they demandingly shout for bread and games, which Aldous Huxley has translated into the language of our century as: "Give me television and hamburgers, but don't bother me with [your talk about] the responsibilities of liberty." The addiction to entertainment is the dangerous antithesis to joy achieved through creative play. The completely passive mental attitude that this state of inaction and nonparticipation aids and abets is not only indicative of an exhausted human, it is just as characteristic of one who is satiated, not to say overstuffed.

The lives of our early ancestors were made up of sequences of experiences that were sometimes full of woe or at least were wearisome and that were then, at other times, accompanied by joy and pleasure. One must have suffered real hunger at least once in order to be able accurately to estimate what joy the acquisition of a great amount of good food can give someone near starvation. The mechanism of the pleasure-nonpleasure experience-economy originally had the function, for animals living in the wild, of weighing the costs of a particular behavior pattern or undertaking against the reward that would be achieved by such action. In order to get hold of a tempting prey, a predacious animal will do many things that give it no pleasure and that, without a subsequent reward, would serve to decondition such behavior. The animal runs through thorn thickets, jumps into cold water and exposes itself to dangers that it demonstrably would otherwise fear. But the proportion of the nonpleasurably accented stimulus situation must stand in a reasonable relationship to the reward. A wolf may not go out hunting during the cold, stormy night of a polar winter oblivious of the influences of the weather: the animal cannot afford to pay for a meal with a frozen toe. Only under circumstances describable as extreme, when, for example, an animal is near starvation, can it become economically advisable to take such a risk, since survival would then depend on getting something to eat. I have presented the functions and capacities of this vital mechanism that adapts behavior to the prevailing "economic situation" of the organism more completely in *Civilized Man's Eight Deadly Sins*. Attached to this apparatus of the pleasure-nonpleasure principle are two fundamental characteristics that we know from virtually all complicated neurosensory mechanisms: the first is the widespread process of habituation, and the second is that of inertia. Habituation occurs when the stimulus situation appears so often it loses its effect; reaction inertia, on the other hand, results in oscillations occurring within the system. When incoming stimuli that produce strong nonpleasure (extreme discomfort, even pain) suddenly let up, the system does not return in a muted curve to its initial state of indifference but, instead, shoots beyond this "established value," this state of quiescence, and registers the cessation of nonpleasure as a marked pleasure and not just the *absence* of discomfort or pain. Almost all of us have experienced how wonderful it is when a tooth stops aching or even when the pain eases off just a little.

Under the conditions that prevailed during the early ages of our human ancestors, life was hard. As hunters and carnivores they were most certainly almost always hungry, and it was no vice for them at all, but a virtue, to eat their fill to the point of bursting when at last a large animal had been bagged. Similar assessments can be made for other behavior norms that are judged nowadays as not being virtues, as even being regarded as deadly sins. To illustrate what I mean: the life led by early humans was so dangerous that cowardice was a virtue, and economizing on muscular exertion, that is, laziness, was too. As early as the dim prehistoric period, however, when things for humans were going only a little better, sages had begun to recognize accurately that it was not all that good when humans were too consistently successful in their strivings to achieve pleasure and to avoid the nonpleasurable. Today modern technological advances and especially the developments made in pharmacology help the human elude the nonpleasurable in ways that did not exist before, ways equatable with subterfuges. In the section covering taming and training methods used by the technocratic system, I discussed how easily we become slaves to modern comfort and ease through coddling and pampering.

From all appearances, young people going through the stages of puberty are especially plagued by boredom. Helmut Qualtinger has written words to the point for the desperation felt by bored youth in his first-rate cabaret song *"Die Halbstarken Rhapsodie"* [The Hippie Rhapsody]: *"Was kann denn i dafur, daß i a so vül Zeit hab, was kann denn i dafur, daß i mit nix a Freid hab"* [It's no fault of mine that I've got so much time on my hands, it's no fault of mine that I don't enjoy anything], and so on. The refrain of this tragic lyric is *"denn dann is uns faaaad"* [because then we are borrrred]. It is a well-known fact to psychiatrists that boredom alone suffices as a motive for suicide. Paradoxically, a severe permanent injury incurred through an attempted suicide leads, in some cases, to a revitalization of individual emotional life and involvement. An experienced Viennese teacher of the blind once told me that he knows several young people who, intending to kill themselves, shot themselves in the temple and, succeeding not in suicide but in injuring the optic-nerve junction, became blind. None of them attempted suicide a second time; not only did they go on living, they also astonishingly matured into balanced, even happy human beings. Similar developments are known for people who have survived their suicide attempts as cripples paralyzed from the waist down. Apparently obstacles difficult to overcome are necessary so that, to these young people bored with the world and despairing, life can once again be allowed to appear meaningful. The educator Kurt Hahn devised a method to demonstrate drastically to blasé and bored young people devoid of hope and full of a sense of futility how worthwhile life is: he organized them into teams of lifeguards; acting on their own, personal initiative and at considerable danger to themselves, they were provided with opportunities to save the lives of others. Independently of Hahn and his method, the psychiatrist Helmut Schulze worked out a procedure through which the value of life could be brought directly before the eyes of his patients; he put them in genuinely threatening, so-called borderline situations in which the patients had good reason to fear for their lives. The transitory success of these methods has been considerable. How far they can permanently counteract feelings of boredom, the draining away of any meaning in this world, of emotional entropy, remains to be seen.

Perhaps these futile feelings of meaninglessness arise in many young people because they have never had the chance to see and experience how *beautiful* organic creation is. The perception of beauty and of harmonies requires schooling. It is possible that such perception belongs to those behavior norms which, as discussed in chapter 10, at their maturation must be put to use and exercised at once if they are not to become irrevocably atrophied through inactivity and nonuse. Young people who grow up in the overcrowded center of a large modern metropolis have little opportunity to get to know anything about the beauty and harmony of organic creation. Added to this, they are bored, time hangs heavy on their hands, they see quite precisely in the lives of their parents how one should not be going about doing this, and are as well, perhaps through hospitalism or through other bonding disturbances incurred while growing up, impaired in their capacities for human love. Who can be surprised when they become cynics and gainsay any meaning to life? It is not only forgivable but a logical consequence when young people who have become convinced of the meaninglessness of the present-day world "want out" of their societies and do, in fact, drop out. Those who drop out in search of alternative ways of living know something fundamentally true that those who are responsible and those who are powerful in this world do not know or, at least, choose not to believe: these young people see that the economic and political behavior of those in power leads to spoilage and ruin. One cannot resent their renunciation of society if they believe that today's social order is the only one possible — and if this were so, the world would actually be meaningless. I feel certain, however, that those who drop out because of such a belief will come to realize that this is an error, and I am convinced that the inherent human need for responsibility and for the freedom to choose can suddenly force open the way that will permit us to strike out in a new direction that encompasses an earnest search for new social forms.

The opposite of an error is often not the truth but, instead, an apposed error. When representatives of the "establishment" are captives of ontological reductionism and technocratic habits of thought, an apposed error is signified when many young people today choose to despise the intellect, turn away from reality and turn toward the mystical beliefs of sects. The extent of mass indoctrination has already reached the limits tolerable by reasoned processes of thought. It is now completely conceivable that what seems, at first, to be an accumulation of merely insignificant insights can begin to set in motion a turning of the tide in what is generally believed by a majority of people. In an optimistic manner, I believe that this process of veering around has already begun.

·⫶⟨ TWELVE ⟩⫶·

Justification
for Optimism

At the outset of our joint venture it was stated that the overall task of this book was to comprehend the waning of what is humane as a complex of symptoms such as those associated with a disease and to search for causes and countermeasures. As professionally responsible physicians, we are obligated morally to act as if we were optimists. For such optimism we also have some justification. But besides being in extreme danger of committing suicide with the help of its nuclear, biological and chemical weapons, mankind is also actually well on the way toward losing all those characteristics, capacities and capabilities that mean being truly human. Even if mankind's swift suicide can somehow be avoided, still there, threatening every one of us, is a world order that has ceased to be humane. Yet clear indications exist and are discernible that a saving countermovement is under way. As is well known, public opinion is subject to oscillations, and I believe that the culmination point of technocratic development has been surpassed. In the previous chapter I have already noted that a changeover has been heralded by today's young people whose points of view can lead back to sound thinking.

What humans regard as real is, as has been emphasized, largely determined by the cultural tradition in which they are reared. This "social construction of reality" (Berger and Luckmann) is related to what we ethologists call imprinting, insofar as its consequences can only with difficulty, or in some cases cannot, be reversed at all. There exists, thus, little hope of convincing those humans who have absorbed the values of the technocratic system from early youth onward that, by expressly these values that they hold, mankind is being herded and driven with steadily increasing speed toward the abyss of inhumanity. This fact has been recognized and completely comprehended by a majority of young people. The proportion of older people sharing their convictions is smaller; abandoning the values of the technocratic society and being prepared to accept new values is, for older humans and because of the reasons cited above, difficult to achieve. Accruing to this condition are the compelling circumstances of everyday life in a technocracy, the daily compulsions that prevent those who are caught up in the competitive conflict from having any long-range view of the future. Therefore the hope that my arguments might be heard rests squarely on the receptivity of young people.

We should not forget how recent are our insights into the existing threats to mankind. I can illustrate this by giving a summary of the development of my own thinking as a scientist; prior to the relatively recent past, not even someone primarily concerned with biology had any clear idea about the pressing dangers. As I have already mentioned, I was not at all convinced by William Vogt's preachings against careless disturbances of ecological states of equilibrium; the world appeared to me then to be still inexhaustibly immense, and William Vogt appeared to be the kind of person we in Austria describe as a *Miesmacher* — an inveterate fault-finder, someone who bad-mouths everything. Essentially, it was Rachel Carson's book *Silent Spring* that caught my attention and roused me to take part in the combat against technocracy.

My sudden discernment of the danger arose, as realizations so often do, through the sudden materialization of a thought connection. All at once I saw the close relationship between the typical neuroses I knew so well and the epidemic spread of the neurotic, hectic way of life of civilized humanity. In a flash it became clear to me how a naive belief in progress, how overorganization, the concentration in metropolitan centers of masses of humans, in short, how all the processes discussed in chapters 7 and 8 of this book combine to form a vast vicious cycle of positive feedback and how close the connections actually are between the waning of humaneness and the mounting self-destructiveness of mankind. The knowledge of neuroses I acquired as a physician during the Second World War contributed to my being able suddenly to see in the waning of those characteristics and capabilities that constitute humanity *symptoms of disease* that I then diagnosed in *Civilized Man's Eight Deadly Sins*.

As short as the elapsed time seems to be since that book made its appearance, what was said there now gives me the impression of being rather dated; what disturbs me most of all is the tone of the message: it is that of the lonely prophet crying out in the wilderness. In view of the many books published since then, the authors of which have strived to get across similar or related warnings, this tone has the effect of being extraordinarily arrogant — it promotes the impression that I am standing isolated with my knowledge, alone on a broad expanse of open country. In reality, the number of people who are clearly aware of the dangers threatening all of mankind has increased significantly, and this number continues to increase, I believe, in a steadily, ever more steeply rising curve. It is to be hoped that the number will grow to include a majority of all humans who recognize the threats that exist to humankind as a species and, above all, the threats that exist to their own humaneness, before we have obstructed the possibilities of achieving a social order that is more human than the one we now have.

One reason for optimism that I can identify is the *oscillation* in public opinion. The single-minded belief in the beatific effect of measuring and counting has, in fact, conferred on mankind a power that had not existed before, but the recognition that this power is not a perfect godsend is beginning to break through. Philosophers who are to be taken seriously have already begun to express themselves, and, as mentioned in chapter 6, what they are saying is that the natural sciences as such have gone off in wrong directions. Even when these humanists go too far, sometimes shooting beyond the mark, they have still contributed very substantially to the resistance being leveled not only against economic growth and the exploitation of nuclear energy, but also against the technocratic system itself. If one extrapolates this curve of cognition, then the hope grows that the opinions held by the public are swinging back. I believe that I can already notice how the perception, however unconscious, of all the essential points discussed here is increasing irresistibly and spreading underground, as it were.

ACHIEVABLE GOALS OF EDUCATION

Since our hopes for such a veering around and return of opinion are, as stated, aligned toward the younger generations, it would behoove us to take effective measures for counteracting the ruinous influences of the technocratic social order on the education of our children and children's children. Our first and most pressing concern should be the prevention of *all* hospitalism. It remains an open question whether there is not an entire series of other human capacities that, in a like manner, waste away when, during a specific critical phase of individual development, they are not put to use. The human is, as Arnold Gehlen has said, *"von Natur aus ein Kulturwesen"* [by nature a cultural creature]. The human receptivity for harmonies, discussed in chapter 9, must also be addressed and awakened at the right time and then used. As I have already mentioned, Gestalt perception, that is, our organ for the perception of harmonies, requires the feeding in of a vast amount of data if it is to be able to fulfill its function. A vital function of education is the presentation to maturing humans of sufficiently abundant and varied material facts to make it possible for them to be able to perceive at all the values associated with the beautiful and the ugly, the good and the bad, the healthy and the sick.

The best school at which young people can learn that the world has significance and meaning is direct contact and association with nature itself. I cannot imagine a normally endowed human child who is allowed close and familiar contact with live creatures, that is, with embodiments of the grand harmonies of nature, being able to perceive the world as meaningless. In establishing this contact it makes no difference with which creature the child enters into a trusting, personal relationship. Owning an animal, caring for it and also bearing the responsibility for its well-being would make any number of children happy. Such simple means are all we need in order to plant in human hearts the joy to be found in creation and in its beauty. Together with the joy discoverable in living creation emerges, as I choose to maintain, within every human child at all capable of any deeper feelings, a *love* for all living creatures. *"Ich liebe, was da lebt"* [I love all that lives] says the messiah in Widmann's short drama *Der Heilige und die Tiere* [The saint and the animals]. I maintain that everyone does this, everyone who has been able to see and experience enough of organic creation.

The magnificence and the beauty of this world must indeed be made readily accessible to the young people of today so that they are not left in any doubt about the present position of mankind and so that they are not left to despair. It can be gauged as a symptom of wanting to get away from it all, as an indicator of what is called escapism, when today's young people choose to turn from all that is rational and reasonable, when some of them take psychedelic drugs or even lapse into drug addiction. It must somehow still be possible to make comprehensible to such young people that truth, too, is not only beautiful but also full of mind-boggling mystery, that one does not have to take drugs or become a mystic in order to experience the wondrous.

At a time when it has become fashionable to regard science as an essentially value-indifferent undertaking, it is understandable that the scientist feels obliged to demand of himself a value-free attitude toward his research subject or toward the object of his study. I regard this vogue as dangerous, however, because of its self-deception. For example, all of the biologists I know are undeniably lovers of their objects of study, in exactly the same sense that someone whose hobby is aquaria is in love with the objects being cared for.

Every human who can become sentient to and experience joy in creation and its beauty is made immune to any and every doubt about its *meaning*. Questions relating to the meaning of organic creation then appear to be just as incomprehensible as similar questions about the meaning of Beethoven's Ninth Symphony appear to someone who loves music. Anyone putting such questions has obviously never had the opportunity to gather up and assimilate within himself as much as is necessary from the grand harmonies of this world for a Gestalt perception to have been made available. For an adequate development of most of the other cognitive capacities of humans, but above all for Gestalt perception, I believe that early childhood experiences are essential.

Speaking or writing about the beauties of the cosmos is a pleonasm since beauty, order and harmony are already subsumed in the meaning of the word *cosmos*. Close acquaintance with the beautiful precludes the erroneous belief, discussed in chapter 5, that only what can be exactly defined and neatly quantified is real.

Lately there have been many philosophical discussions about the "meaning of meaning." Two scholars at Oxford even wrote a book called *The Meaning of Meaning*. It should actually be the responsibility of a healthy rearing and a real education to impart to the maturing human the realization that it is most certainly possible to differentiate the meaningful from the meaningless. We possess a well-grounded and richly endowed fund of factual material on the basis of which one is justified in making judgmental statements about when a linguistic symbol, for example, is being used correctly and when its use is false. Despite this possession and possibility, children and young people are never taught the ways in which truth can be distinguished from falsity, the senseless separated from the significant and meaningful. Yet one can do this! That this is not done, that this most momentous and, for freedom in human thinking, so exceedingly important aspect is neglected in the rearing and educating of our children, that this theme is not taught as a predominant part of every school curriculum is deplorable.

Those with power in the overpopulated and overorganized world will go on using all of the already known and many new techniques for manipulating humans and for reducing them to the lowest common level. It should be feared that those in power also will not hesitate to reinforce these measures of nonrational persuasion by means of economic coercion, even by threats of force. If we want to prevent the sort of tyranny that, independent of every political orientation, develops when the size of a nation-state reaches specific dimensions, we must begin at once to make our children immune to manipulations of their emotional and intellectual development. This immunization can only be achieved when every maturing human has been taught thoroughly to see through the techniques of propaganda.

We have become so accustomed to the usual propaganda methods used in our own society that we have acquired a dangerous tolerance for empty promises and other institutionalized forms of the common lie. But when we come into contact with the dictates of political systems other than our own, we notice at once the straitjacket into which the subject citizens are strapped. How very much the same is true for ourselves, for our "democratic" forms of government, we overlook all too easily. Once when attending a scientific congress in Weimar, in East Germany, I found the absence of all neon signs and other lighted advertisements extraordinarily praiseworthy and agreeable. By way of contrast, I was vexed by the omnipresent cloth banners on which the friendship with the Soviet Union, the community of interests that united all human workers of the world, and other such slogans were proclaimed. Back then, in Weimar, it was suddenly clear to me that the socialist-communist banners and the Western advertisements in lights were analogous organs of two different sovereign systems set up for maintaining control. At the same time I began to understand how uncommonly difficult it is to oppose a doctrine without, while doing this, becoming the captive of a counterdoctrine.

A large-scale attempt to initiate just such an opposition miscarried during the thirties of this century. A prominent philanthropist named Filene established an Institute for Propaganda Analysis in 1937 at a time when national socialist propaganda began insinuating itself into the United States. Analyses made at the institute concentrated on propaganda designed especially to appeal not to understanding and comprehending but to the emotions, and several studies were carried out in which high school and college students were used to clarify the essential nature of this kind of advertising. Then the war broke out, and since the allied governments also set up bureaus propagating unrestrained "psychological warfare," the desire to analyze this type of propaganda began to seem emphatically tactless. But even before the outbreak of the war there were many who found the activities of the institute most objectionable and undesirable. Certain educators, for example, concluded that analyses of advertising methods would make maturing humans cynical in ways that were not wanted. Just as unwelcome was any acquisition of insight into the propaganda methods of the higher military authorities; they feared that recruits might begin to analyze pronouncements made by the officers responsible for their training. Religious authorities were opposed to propaganda analysis because this activity could undermine beliefs and reduce the number of people attending church services. Experts at advertising agencies protested because propaganda analysis could undercut loyalty to a particular product and lower the sales figures. The institute was closed down.

All attempts to immunize young people against the stratagems of advertising are threatened by the great danger that the devil will be driven out by promoting Beelzebub: it can happen even to the well-intentioned that the doctrine they wish to fight against is opposed by one that turns out to be just as rigid and paralyzing. A grandiose and sensible and honestly intentioned attempt to formulate a philosophy of nonindoctrinability went tragically on the rocks: the philosophy of dialectical materialism was fashioned by Karl Marx with the purpose of imparting to mankind a world view that would be capable of protecting itself against the danger of ever petrifying into a doctrine. In a transformation derived from the teachings of Hegel, Karl Marx professed that the antithesis, that is, the point of view opposing the predominating opinion, is initially to be considered as the more correct. It is in fact one of the greatest tasks a researcher seeking truth has — preserving the readiness to dismantle and restructure all held hypotheses. Despite the best intentions of its creator, out of dialectical materialism has come the most petrified of all doctrines and probably the most powerful that has ever prevailed on earth.

The political opponents of Filene's propaganda analyses entered the lists in their time with the argument that these studies would seduce young people into complete cynicism and skepticism, and the argument does in fact contain a kernel of truth.

Healthy skepticism is indispensable if the intention is to distinguish the correct from the false, the lie from the truth, but an exaggeration of the skeptical attitude can actually lead to cynicism and the disavowal of all values. The education and training for perceiving the grand harmonies discussed in the previous section, learning how to perceive the beautiful as well as the good, are absolutely necessary in order that a balanced view of our grandiose world can be transmitted to young people. A person smitten by a bad case of ontological reductionism or scientism could, through a one-sided education emphasizing propaganda analysis, be induced simply to doubt everything and also be brought to despair.

When one attempts to make the beauty and grandeur of this world perceptibly concrete for maturing young people, one certainly hopes at the same time to rouse their interests in the world's inner relationships. The wish that Faust summarizes with the words "*daß ich erkenne, was die Welt im Innersten zusammenhält*" [that I may comprehend what holds the core of the world together] expresses a general human need that in some people is stronger, in other people weaker. (Among natural scientists this need becomes a life-dominating motive.) A complete lack of curiosity signifies an abnormality.

I nourish the supposition that the rousing of curiosity could possibly also lead to a revitalization of lost interhuman involvement and concern. In the Parsifal epic and in the sagas forming the basis of the poem, it is reckoned as an onerous sin that the hero is present during the sufferings of Amfortas, king of the knights of the Holy Grail, that he looks on but does not ask the reason or cause of such agony. Perhaps in what inspired this scene is to be found a presentiment of the connection that exists between the interest humans have for the world in general and the sympathy and concern they have for their fellow humans. Perhaps it is possible that through rousing interest in the extensive connections extant within nature, sympathy and concern for the lives of one's fellow humans could also be stirred awake.

In order to reveal to young people the spectacular diversity of organic creation and, at the same time, its regularity and orderliness, one needs to make them familiar with one of the larger animal or plant groups. Collecting and describing what is collected, something that is so denigrated in so many places today, is, I am convinced, the best way to begin to know something about the cosmos, the best way to begin to understand it. Children enjoy collecting; what has been collected quite automatically suggests arrangement and classification in some proper order. When some order has actually been achieved, the resulting arrangement asks for an explanation. What has been accomplished then is what occurs in the development of every natural science — the systematic stage derived from the descriptive stage and the nomothetic stages based on the systematic stage.

Everything living has — in Nicolai Hartmann's sense — a categorically higher form of being than every kind of non-living material. Nevertheless, everything living has the existence of that form of material as a prerequisite. Since all living systems are continuously threatened by disturbances that can come from inside as well as from outside the system, everything living is threatened by sickness and death. Because, like all other organisms, we must constantly defend ourselves against threats of all kinds, we are programmed in such a way that we fear death much more intensely than the very real awfulness of our dying warrants. Great courage is required in order to be able *"nach jenem engen Durchgang hinzustreben, um dessen Mund die ganze Hölle flammt, zu diesem Schritt sich heiter zu entschließen, und sei es mit Gefahr, ins Nichts dahinzufließen"* [to strive to reach that narrow passage, around whose threshold all hell flames, to decide to take this step serenely, accompanied by danger though it is, and to flow out into nothingness].

Although this flowing out into nothingness is completely

unavoidable for those of us who do not believe in a life to come, we still make every effort to postpone the passage as long as possible. In fact the Hippocratic oath obligates those of us who are physicians to do just this for our fellow humans. And for this reason we are also duty-bound to recognize illnesses as early as possible. But the cognitive capacity that makes it possible for us to do this is identical with the capacity already discussed that makes the grand harmonies of the universe accessible to all of us, namely, Gestalt perception.

No matter how familiar to us the concept of sickness may be, we are still not able to define it with any ease. If one says that sickness is a disturbance of the normal harmony of a living system, this definition seems unsatisfactory in that "normal" and "disturbed" can be defined only with reference to a quite specific environmental situation. (The example used earlier was the inherited anomaly of the red blood cells known as sickle-cell anemia.) In Gambia one had to, or to put it more exactly, at one time one had to have this inherited illness in order to remain "healthy." The same principle can be applied to the most diverse environments.

Notwithstanding this limitation to our concept formation, each one of us still knows and perceives quite accurately and correctly what a healthy living system is and what a sick living system is. The capacity for perceiving the scale gradations that lead from the healthy to the sick has as a prerequisite, just as the perception of musical harmonies has, that prior to perception and in preparation for this a considerable trove of factual material is gathered in and accumulated. With the function being discussed here, the wondrous capability of Gestalt perception is revealed with special impressiveness: the collection of an unbelievably large number of single facts and, at the same time, the realization of innumerable interrelationships existing among these facts, and the storing of all of this over a long period of time. The diagnostic faculties of the physician, the skills of the person who takes care of animals and the most essential capabilities of the ecologist are to be found in their looking at a living system and, purely perceptually and, initially, without deliberation or reflection, being able to see that in the system something is awry. This accomplishment is the very same one known as the "clinical eye" of the experienced physician. One of the greatest disservices the scientistic way of thinking has rendered humanity is evidenced in the present-day training of medical doctors during which too little weight or none at all is placed on the development of the "clinical eye." It is a delusional hope that one can ever replace this capacity of our perception through accumulating and storing an enormous amount of data and programming for their possible interrelationships by means of computers.

The success of those who take care of animals is also extensively dependent on perceiving the smallest, the most minute change in the state of health of these charges and being able to bring the measures taken for their care into a proper relationship with such changes. This accomplishment of "bringing into relationship" is obviously, once again, a nonrational accomplishment of Gestalt perception.

It must still, in some way, be possible to provide even those children born and reared in large cities with some kind of opportunity for developing their capacities to perceive the harmony and disharmony of living systems — if only by means of an aquarium. Those children who are given a chance to tend an aquarium and to care for its inhabitants come to learn, through necessity, to comprehend a functioning entirety in its harmony and disharmony, an entirety bringing together and combining very many systems consisting of animals, plants, bacteria and an entire range of inorganic givens, systems that complement one another and systems that are antagonistic to one another. Children would learn how delicate the equilibrium of such an artificial ecological system is. An aquarium presents an *in vitro* model of a natural environment and, by doing this, can awaken the sensitivities of young observers to the significance inherent in the interrelationships of living systems.

Educating our children to perceive the beautiful and the harmonious, to recognize the disharmonies of sick systems and to be antipathetic toward indoctrination is certainly one effective measure that could be taken against the increasing dehumanization of Western civilization. Even more important, it seems to me, would be the awakening in our children (and in ourselves) of sympathy and compassion for all of our fellow creatures. Compassion motivates that sort of love for everything there is that lives to which Albert Schweitzer conferred such moving expression.

The grand harmonious accords of living creation contain, of necessity, a great number of dissonances that we are in the habit of "not hearing"; we tend to repress and to displace them in the psychoanalytic sense, that is, we exclude them from our conscious minds, or we retouch and rework them to improve them. The worst of these dissonances is the need to kill, a necessity that exists not only for the specialized beast of prey but also for us humans. (The words themselves — "prey" and "predacious" and "predatory" with their original meanings of "spoil" and "booty" and "living by preying on others" — incorporate unacceptable analogies — robbery and fraud — to human behavior; the identifications should probably be phrased as "beasts of the chase" or "game animals" or "hunting animals.") Just because of my close friendship with my dogs I always suffer a severe shock whenever they have, once again, bagged a cat — however desirable it might be to keep our garden free of cats for the sake of the extensive population of songbirds there. I also admit that I cannot even watch when a film or television program shows how a predacious animal kills its prey. Darwin reports that when, during the journey on board H.M.S. *Beagle*, he came to be within a tropical forest for the first time, he saw a spider-killing giant wasp attack a bird spider. What did the great naturalist do? Did he take out his pocket watch, his notebook and his pencil and observe closely the process that, at the time, was already known in broad outline, during which the wasp paralyzes the spider by means of a stab into the mass of ganglion nerve tissue and then drags it, still alive, into a nest cavern as food for its larva? No! Charles Darwin drove the wasp away, although he certainly must have been interested in witnessing the behavior sequences precisely.

Compassion for suffering creatures is an unequivocal, qualitative, indicative emotion denoting real sorrow felt by all sensitive people, despite their insightful acknowledgment that both the suffering and the death of individual living beings are unavoidable within the grand harmonies of living creation. It does not help us or our feelings in the least to know all about the harmonious interrelationships that exist between predacious animal species and their prey animals. It also does not help us very much when we tell ourselves that it would not be doing the prey animals, as species, any favor at all if the animals that hunted them were to disappear from the stage of living actors — as some sentimental lovers of animals, in their incomprehension of natural systems, often wish could happen. We should not disavow the sorrow and pain that accrue to us through compassion. We should also admit to ourselves that we often take sides in equal measure, sometimes rooting for the hunter and sometimes for the hunted. A miniature weasel is one of the most enchanting creatures alive; its movements when at play are captivatingly graceful, although these very same movements are used in earnest when it comes to hunting and killing. A yellow-necked field mouse is hardly any less lovable than a miniature weasel, and when we see how the clever, instinctive movements of the miniature weasel, which have just charmed us so while it played, are now going to be employed seriously to put an end to the yellow-necked field mouse — large-eyed and sensitive and most certainly very capable of suffering — we stand before this dissonance with rent hearts. At least I do; I own to being deeply shocked. At the same time I would probably be quite capable of killing a yellow-necked field mouse myself if I had in my care a half-starved miniature weasel.

In the grand harmony of the living world compassion plays no real role. Suffering is incomparably much older than is commiseration with suffering; suffering came into the world when creatures became capable of subjective experience and with their realization of the inevitable death that awaits each individual — many millions of years before compassion became a part of consciousness. Indications of compassion are already present among chimpanzees. Jane van Lawick-Goodall reports that a female chimpanzee stayed for days with her dying mother, chasing the flies away. When the mother finally died, the daughter listened at the mother's chest and afterward left the corpse, probably because she no longer heard a heartbeat. Compassion felt for living beings not belonging to one's own species assuredly is to be found only among humans.

Originally sympathy was most certainly present only when one individual was bonded to another by love. Love for what lives is an important, indispensable emotion. This emotion is what places the burden of responsibility for all life on our planet squarely upon humans who are sovereign over all of it. The responsible human being may not push aside or repress awareness of the suffering endured by other creatures and least of all the suffering sustained by fellow humans. With this responsibility the human is confronted by a most difficult task.

The quality of feeling inherent in sympathy and compassion, and the readiness to help and the willingness to intervene in the course things take, which go along with that quality, most probably came into being during the evolution of humans together with those behavior norms that emerged to serve parental care; these were later enlarged to include other fellow humans and, when expanded once again, to encompass other living beings. A minimal diminution in the selectivity of the releasing mechanisms involved would be sufficient to cause this to happen.

As important as it is to awaken in humans their sympathy for all living beings dwelling together with us on the earth, and as indispensable as an understanding of that love for what lives may be, we must still make an incisive separation between our feelings for animals and those we have for our fellow humans. We cannot in fact watch, without being inwardly torn, while a mother cheetah brings her ravishingly sweet kittens, as plunder, a just as sweet baby Thompson gazelle that is still alive in order to be able to teach the cheetah children how to kill; it is not within our powers to rechannel the currents of nature and to prevent cheetahs from eating Thompson gazelles, or miniature weasels from devouring yellow-necked field mice.

But what is most definitely not an irreversible current flowing through the organic world is the circumstance that the greatest portion of mankind lives in want while a small portion is plagued by the consequences of gluttony, consuming as well as food more than seventy percent of the energy that is available for all of mankind.

A thinking and feeling human could not bear the inescapably cruel dissonances within the great living systems were he not capable, periodically, of pushing the thoughts about such brutalities to the side. I would most likely become a vegetarian if I myself were forced to butcher everything living that serves me as nourishment. Here it is permissible for the human to repress, and, in fact, he must. But in cases concerning avoidable suffering, above all the preventable suffering of fellow human beings, *repression is not permissible*. Repressing compassion, turning away from the suffering of animals, can become dangerous because it can become habitual. In the course of time one learns all too well to look away and, while doing this, to turn off one's feelings of compassion, also when this is not permissible — in those instances where one can help. After what has just been said it will be clear that I regard as a great service the initiatives undertaken by societies established for the protection of animals, and how highly I value the work done by those who, through word and by deed, have gone into action against the so-called close herding and battery caging of domestic animals. Yet I still have a nagging suspicion that the amount of compassion many humans can feel for animals stands in an inverse ratio to the love they can express for their fellow human beings. It would not be uninteresting to know if there are more people who commit themselves, or even contribute, to causes concerned with animal protection than commit themselves or contribute to Amnesty International. I hope the proportions never confirm my suspicion.

THOU SHALT NOT BEAR FALSE WITNESS

Das Schlimmste aber ist das falsche Wort, die Lüge
Wär' nur der Mensch erst wahr, er wär auch gut.
Wie könnte Sünde irgend doch besteh'n,
wenn sie nicht lügen könnte, täuschen?
Erst sich, alsdann die Welt, dann Gott, ging es nur an.
Gäb's einen Bösewicht, müßt' er sich sagen,
so oft er nur allein: Du bist ein Schurk'!
Wer hielt' sie aus, die eigene Verachtung.

[The worst, though, is the false word, the lie / Were humans only truthful, they would be good as well. / How then could sin exist at all / if they could not lie, deceive? / First themselves, then the world, then God only would be involved. / Were there a scoundrel, he needs must say to himself /whenever he was alone: You're a knave! / Who could endure it, one's own disdain.]

This is what Franz Grillparzer has the Bishop of Chalon declaim in his drama *Weh' dem, der lügt* [Woe to them who lie]. One can define a lie as the conscious issuance of false information that secures for the sender advantages over the receiver. ("White" lies that are not motivated by selfishness do not form a part of this discussion.) Sending out false information is a strategy that is common at a very much simpler, unconscious level. Already in the plant kingdom there are flower forms that "pretend" to be female insects of a particular species and, by inciting the males of this species to "copulate," these plants promote their own propagation. A great deal of what is called mimicry deceives the receiver of the signals to the advantage of the sender. A classic example of this is the imitating of a cleaner wrasse (*Labroides dimidiatus*) by the blenny Aspidontus. The latter simulates the cleaner wrasse not only in color and form down

to the smallest detail, it also imitates the characteristic movements the cleaner wrasse uses to encourage its clients to
hold still and to present portions of their bodies for cleaning.
While in the case of the lying and thieving blenny the prey
is "bamboozled" into being bit, in a great majority of cases
the strategy is the reverse, mimicry for defense rather than
attack. Caterpillars simulate the heads of snakes by means
of a pair of eyes "painted" on their first body segments;
many other insects also show pairs of eyes which, when
displayed at appropriate distances, deceive an approaching
predator into believing that it is being faced by a larger
vertebrate. The most widely dispersed misinformation that
potential prey animals send out to advancing enemies tends
to be that of making oneself appear larger than one really
is: spreading out the arms and the fin edges among the
cephalopods and the fishes; bristling or ruffling the fur or
the plumage among warm-blooded animals; and the inflating
and distending of the lungs among reptiles and amphibians
are all well known.

Perhaps the reader will have noticed that, in all of the
examples cited, the information sent out was not sent to a
member of one's own species. One might at first believe
that a fish threatening a rival by means of broadside display
manifestations, which include making oneself as large as
possible, is also doing this in an effort to "bluff," that is, in
an endeavor to make his fighting potential appear greater
than it actually is. Amotz Zahavi has marshaled convincing
arguments for his thesis that signals and releasing movements which have evolved through their effect on conspecifics must possess, of necessity, a high degree of reliability,
that is to say, of "honesty." Especially for those signals that
are determinant for sexually selective breeding, a certain
guarantee must be present that the signal sent correlates

with the actual qualities possessed by the sender. On this reliability is based the great uniformity and standardization of characteristics that are determinant for sexually selective breeding. Similar to the most precisely standardized conditions established for testing the competitors in sports contests so that the qualitative differences among them are permitted to appear, are, for example, the exactly standardized nuptial "clothes" worn by all male mallards, and also the behavior patterns exhibited during courtship by all graylag ganders. In just this way do the small differences existing among the individuals come to light for the discriminating human observer and, of course, for the conspecific as well. Without having to fall back upon references to group selection and phylum selection, one has enough of an argument here to assert that in signal exchanges between and among conspecifics there is no faking or lying.

Since, however, there most certainly are, in addition, both group selection and consanguineous selection, and since the releaser and the inborn releasing mechanism — the sender and the receiver of species-internal signals — are complementary organs within a species-confined system, one may assume without further ado that, as I maintained in 1966, the releaser and the inborn releasing mechanism exert a selection pressure on one another. This also speaks for the assumption that conspecifics do not "lie" to one another. Said in another way: the vital interests of an animal species are furthered best by incorrectly informing prey or the marauding enemy, but not the conspecific. The possibility for lying in the literal sense appears to have been first provided by language. Because of this it cannot be at all astonishing that, among humans, the so very common practice of lying to one's conspecifics gives rise to such evil consequences for human society and for the human species. Only the individual alone can derive advantages from lying — at the price, to be sure, of becoming a parasite on the society.

While the lie is not known to the genetically programmed mechanisms for signal exchanges among animals within a species, there is in some higher mammals an individually learned and perhaps insightful behavior indicative of a rudimentary form of lying. Georg Rüppell has told me about a female arctic fox that would free herself for a time from her pups by means of a fraudulent maneuver whenever they began to pester her too much: she would bark out the warning yap and, in response, her children would hurl themselves head over heels back into the lair while she herself gave no further indications of being alarmed.

A very remarkable story about an old male orangutan was told to me by A. F. J. Portielje, at the time the director of the Artis Zoological Gardens in Amsterdam. This orangutan did not lie, but he was, instead, lied to, and threw himself into a most violent fit of fury because of this. At the zoological gardens he occupied a cage that had rather restricted floor space but, as way of compensation, extended up to the ceiling of the rather high building. In order to induce the orangutan to move around enough, he was fed near the floor and his platform for resting was located as high up as it was possible to place it, so that every time he was fed he had to climb down and then climb back up again. Only when the cage needed cleaning was the orangutan fed by a caretaker in the uppermost regions of the cage; the caretaker was forced to climb a stepladder to accomplish this. While the animal was being fed, the floor of the cage was quickly cleaned — a process that in itself was rather easily and swiftly completed. One day, toward the end of such a feeding and cleaning, came the unpleasant surprise: the orangutan dropped down suddenly to the cage floor and before the sliding door of the cage could be closed he had grabbed the edge of the door with one hand and had braced the other against the door jamb. Fortunately Portielje was on hand at the time. While animal caretaker and zoo director tried, with all their strength augmented by desperation, to force the door shut, the powerful arms of the ape slowly and irresistibly widened the opening. It was at this impasse that Portielje had the saving idea which, in view of the tension of the situation, was nothing less than inspired: precipitately he pulled his hands away from the door and, shrieking in terror, jumped back and stared, wild-eyed, with mouth agape, at a point just beyond and behind the back of the orangutan — as if something most terrifying had just appeared there. The orangutan fell for the deception, swung himself around to confront the danger, and the door of the cage was snapped into its lock. What is important about this anecdote is the aftermath. The orangutan flew into a violent rage such as Portielje had never before witnessed in an animal of this species. Portielje told me that he was completely convinced that the orangutan had full insight into the circumstances of the episode and was incensed about having believed a lie. Planned experiments on how anthropoid apes react to being lied to have, as far as I know, never been conducted.

Verbal language naturally provides undreamed of new possibilities for propagating erroneous information.

It is conceivable that the negative valuation of the lie has as a basis innate programs. It is most certainly an evil for human society when its citizen members lie to one another, with the intention of gaining advantages over one another. I believe that the lying done by individual humans evokes in us a negative value perception of a different and other sort than does the lying classifiable as collective, political or economic. The romantic glorification of "Teutonic loyalty," which was still very much a part of the upbringing of my generation, is probably a fabrication of the Roman writer Tacitus, who used Germanic fidelity in his extraordinarily honorable propaganda campaign against the moral degeneracy of the high culture in Rome. It is doubtful that Tacitus knew anything more about the loyalty, fidelity and trustworthiness attributed to the Germanic-speaking tribes than what he had from hearsay. But with certainty one can extract from the writings of Tacitus the fact that, toward the end of the period of Roman high culture, everyone was lying to everyone else nineteen to the dozen.

The biblical commandment against lying is much more conscientiously followed between individual humans than it is between collectives. Every single member of any and every supervisory board has my complete trust, and I would accept his counsel without hesitation; as a collective, however, a supervisory board can act in unscrupulous and amoral ways. Apparently the division of responsibility relieves the individual board member of all responsibility. Despite the incompleteness of our knowledge, I dare to proffer the supposition that the frequency of public and governmental lying and the general tolerance for being lied to have both increased with the development of high cultures and higher civilization. In the commercial transactions of our day haggling and the mendacious praise of products often qualify as thoroughly permissible. Some advertising experts are not only not ashamed of themselves but are proud whenever they achieve success with a lie. I believe in all seriousness that human society as a whole would experience a complete and beneficently reoriented organization if the lie, the personal as well as the collective, were to be assessed as it actually deserves.

VALUES THAT MUST BE REVALUED

I want it to be clear that the directions to be taken in education discussed in a previous section, as measures for countering the waning of the humane, unambiguously strive toward the ambitious goal of reappraising an entire series of values. If I believe that this tremendous task is manageable at all, it is because my optimism is based on the fact that those a prioristic value sensibilities discussed in chapter 6 are, in the most elevated sense of the words, commonly and universally human. They are not dependent on cultural tradition or on the social constructs of reality, about which I wrote in chapter 10. In other words, the senses of values that are being discussed here must not be acquired by humans through inculcation or through the beating of backsides black and blue; they awaken and come to life entirely on their own if the Gestalt perceptions of maturing humans are made familiar with the unadulterated factual material that reveals to us the "cognizant reality of nature."

These are simple perceptions, accessible to healthy human common sense, that remain closed off for so many humans through a split in their thinking for which, I am convinced, the idealistic, or, better expressed, the ideationistic belief, that the real world can contain no values must bear most of the blame. What needs to be made clear here is the simple, straightforward fact that the reality of creation embodies awe-inspiring values and possesses the potential to engender continually still higher values. In our search for the meaning of the world, it is not necessary for us to meander around in the supernatural or in the extranatural. Goethe has Faust say: "*Tor, wer dorthin die Augen blinzelnd richtet, sich über Wolken seinesgleichen dichtet! Er stehe fest und sehe sich hier um! Dem Tüchtigen ist diese Welt nicht stumm.*" [Fool is he who directs his eyes squinting upward, imagining his likeness above the clouds! Stand firm instead and look around here! To the resourceful, this world is not mute.]

THE EPISTEMOLOGICAL STANDPOINT

In the preceding sections I presented a series of recommendations concerning education that would more readily serve the formation of value perceptions than the development of rational thinking. Humans who are capable of seeing how beautiful the world is cannot help but face the world with optimism. The knowledge they acquire about the grandeur and the beauty of creation will help them resist the methods and the messages of today's propaganda and the pressures of indoctrination. The truth inherent in the real world will teach them to bear no false witness against any neighbor. Their perceptibilities for the grand harmonies will become so deeply seated and skilled that they will be capable of differentiating what is sick from what is healthy and not be in despair about the great harmony of organic creation when they experience the tragedies of suffering and death of individual beings.

Those are all things that are self-evident for every human near to nature. To evaluate them accurately requires no intellectual capability, only the "open eyes" conferred by the ratiomorphic, nonrational accomplishments of Gestalt perception. All those who share this kind of world view perceive, unerringly, compassion for their fellow creatures and for the fate of the individual being; together with this compassion love is born for all that is alive and living, and with this love comes the realization of responsibility.

All this is not sentimental illusion, as the adherents of ontological reductionism appear to believe. If I have dedicated the entire second part of this book to the reality of the "merely" subjective, this has been done in order to refute that very error.

Everything written in this book is a consequence of views provided from the theoretical prospect of evolutionary epistemology and the conviction, on the one hand modest and on the other nevertheless self-certain, concerning what this theory of knowledge tells us about ourselves. It weans us radically from that tragic overestimation of ourselves we inherited from ancient Greek culture; it teaches us not to see humans as the adversaries and the opponents of all the rest of nature, as does platonic idealism — better said, platonic ideationism — and as, ultimately, Immanuel Kant's transcendental idealism assumes. But, most important, this evolutionary epistemology also teaches us to regard all of the cognitive accomplishments of humans as functions of real physiological organizations that, in our experiential life, form images of the same actual external world as the one that is brought to us through quantifying ratiocination. *This assessment of the subjective is, however,* as must be most emphatically stated, *the result of rational thinking.*

I maintain that all these in themselves banal perceptions, however seldom they are thought about or even consciously brought to mind, form the basis of the work of all natural scientists who have recognized the significance and implications of the facts of evolution. Rupert Riedl has compared this more or less unconscious spread of new knowledge to the growth of a hyphomycete fungus that branches out below ground and then, at various removed places, pushes up to the surface sporophores that appear, to the superficial observer, to be independent of one another. The ideas that led to an evolutionary epistemology were simultaneously formulated, in apparent independence, by Karl Popper, by Donald Campbell, by Rupert Riedl and by me. Each of us came to his initially summational conclusions along entirely separate routes. Popper reached his results through logic, Campbell through psychology, Riedl through comparative morphology, and I myself through the comparative study of animal behavior. Recently Rupert Riedl discovered that Ludwig Boltzmann had expressed the same ideas as early as a century ago. Boltzmann wrote: "How will one now treat what one calls, in logic, the laws governing thinking [the formal principles of reasoning]? Well, in the Darwinian sense, these laws of thought will be [regarded as] nothing other than inherited habits of thought . . . since, if we did not bring these laws of thought with us [as part of our heredity], all knowing would cease and the [processes of] perception would be without any context." None of us, thus, needs to flatter himself overly much for having arrived at some new aspect of knowledge. Käthe Heinroth, the widow of my great teacher, cited in criticism of the table of contents of this book, what she presumed her husband would probably have said about it: "But every natural scientist already knows all that; one does not have to make an extra-special thing of it." Despite this judgment I am convinced that were Oskar Heinroth alive today, he would express a different point of view. Max Planck wrote to me after reading my first piece of work in which these ideas about the relationship between the observer and the thing observed were written down; it afforded him deep satisfaction, he said, that starting from such different premises, as he and I had done, one could come to such completely corresponding views on the relationship between the real world and the phenomenal world.

Of course Mrs. Heinroth was right; of course everything that is said in this book is actually self-evident, obvious. But just such a banality as the conceptualization of what is human, a conceptualization that the evolutionary theory of cognition allows us to formulate and that I have tried to present in this book, forms the foundation of my hope that the waning of the humane can still be checked. It must — "By Jove!"

as Plato has Socrates say — still be possible to bring them to their senses.

I have always been fascinated by feasibilities for comparing the *Weltbildapparat*, the perceiving apparatus of various animals. Reading Alfred Kühn's classic book *Die Orientierung der Tiere im Raum* [The orientation of animals in space] provided the stimulation to do this. The spatial orientation of animals illustrates beautifully how different are the kinds and the amounts of information gained by various living beings through their spatially oriented reactions. The paramecium "knows" through its escape reaction, the so-called phobic reaction, in which direction its progress is being blocked. Through the so-called topical reaction, also a part of the paramecium's behavior repertoire, the response tack taken by the animal is determined by the angle of incidence to the stimulus location, so that the animal does not turn blindly any which way, but turns instead in the only direction that makes any sense. In this can be seen that the topical reaction incorporates an incomparably greater amount of information than the phobic reaction.

From these most simple forms of a representation of space in the behaviors of the lowest animals a ladder leads, without a rung missing, up to the human form of conceptualized space. By observing the behavior of anthropoid apes we know that, without moving a muscle — unless, perhaps, it is an eye muscle — they can, in a purely "envisaged" space, carry out "imaged" trial runs of action sequences. Such trial actions initiated in the mind within envisaged space can be called, quite simply, *thinking*. When an ape, in this way, through pondering, finds the solution to a problem he or she has been up against and, with a joyous shout and showing complete certainty of success, carries out the action, one has, as an observer, the compelling impression that this animal has just undergone what Karl Bühler termed the "Aha! experience."

If one compares the various envisagings that are traced by the action systems of various living beings, one becomes consciously aware of several essential facts. To begin with, I find it an astonishing fact that nothing the animal knows about the spatial givens of this world is *false*; the information they have is merely incomparably much more rudimentary than the information we have. Even according to the image we have of the world, the information on which the phobic reaction of the paramecium is based is correct: in that direction from which the escape reaction of the animalcule has forced it to veer, it cannot in fact go onward. Often several phobic reactions must be carried out, one after the other, before it finds a route free of obstructions. If one compares the image of the world that simpler creatures have with the image we have, their picture appears to be not incorrect, not distorted, but, as it were, projected onto a coarser "screen" or "grid" that reproduces much less detail — a simile I used more than forty years ago in my article "*Kants Lehre vom Apriorischen im Lichte gegenwärtiger Biologie*" [Kant's theory of the a priori in the light of present-day biology]. In other words, everything animals know about the real external world is *correct!* If one is conscious of being aware, since the earliest phases of childhood, that one is a living being just as an owl or a wild goose is a living being, then one takes it for granted that our own knowledge about the world is just as limited by the confines of the capacities of our world-perceiving apparatus as the knowledge of every other organism is limited by theirs, even when the boundaries of our knowledge are extended incomparably farther. Particularly when comparing the tremendous differences extant among the world-perceiving apparatuses of individual animal forms does one significant fact become clear: all of the incoming messages received by all of these world-perceiving apparatuses pertaining to the same given environment *never contradict one another.* Even the unidimensional spatial view of the paramecium forms an "objective" image of a given of the external world that is also depicted, and in the same way, in our more highly differentiated perceptual picture of the world. In *Behind the Mirror* I argued that the correspondence among the perceived worlds of various humans and, above all, the congruity between and among the perceived worlds of various species of organisms represent a strong argument for the assumption that a uniform extrasubjective reality is being portrayed by all of these incoming messages perceived.

Insight into the fact that everything we know is based on confrontation and interaction between a real perceiving apparatus within us and a just as real world outside us, makes us, at one and the same time, both humble and sure of ourselves. We are made humble because it would be flagrant arrogance to believe that the boundaries of the human perceiving apparatus at the present level of its development are equatable with the boundaries of what is possible to perceive. Even within a time period that, from the standpoint of phylogenesis, is minute, humans have significantly extended the boundaries of the perceivable through the construction of "perception prosthetics." I have already used the capacities of such mechanic-electronic aids as a simile in the mirror book in order to demonstrate how inapt it would be to declare the present boundaries between the perceivable and the imperceptible as final and absolute.

Thus we are not amazed whenever we stumble onto things that cannot be envisaged by the means available to our apparatus, and we are also not amazed that sometimes "double images" can be seen — when, for example, as I have already described, the same real given (an electron) can seem irretrievably dual, particle and wave at once. We are fully aware that, like children in a magic forest, we find ourselves in the middle of sheer endlessness, yet still, in principle, in the midst of a finite fullness of unfathomable mysteries, and we also know that these mysteries lie within that realm where the presiding power is natural creation; that the "mysteries" are "unfathomable" resides in the circumscriptions of our capacities for perception. To quote Carl Zuckmayer's rat catcher once again, "There are natural things we know, and there are unknowable things that are also natural."

Thus evolutionary epistemology compellingly imparts to us that we should not overestimate human beings or their perceptual capacities and, above all, that the unfathomable need not necessarily be something supernatural. But concurrently with a recognition of the boundaries inherent in our faculties for perception comes the confidence in the *realness* of that which our cognitive functions envisage of the extrasubjective reality surrounding us, and this confidence makes us sure of ourselves. If our world-perceiving apparatus came into being through adaptation to this real world, then its present form will have been determined by the selection pressure its envisaging capacity has had placed on it.

From this ensues a very precise positioning of the relationship between the real world and the phenomenal world, a positioning that is, furthermore, identical with the one dictated to us by what we call common sense. I will repeat what I mean using other words and another formulation: *every phenomenon corresponds to something real;* it makes no difference if the phenomenon is a perception of extrasubjective reality, that is, something outside ourselves, or if the phenomenon is perceived through feeling and emotions, as coming from within ourselves. What is real, thus, is not at all only the physically definable and quantitatively verifiable, but also everything sensed and felt. The capability of loving and the capacity for friendship, with all their associated feelings, have come into being in precisely the same way during the course of human phylogenesis as the capabilities for measuring and for counting. *Both* kinds of phenomena draw upon and relate to *the same* reality, a reality to which a feeling and experiencing fellow human belongs just as well as those things that are measurable and countable.

In this I see perhaps the most important consequence of evolutionary epistemology. When we understand and accept the fact that feelings and emotions convey just as valid messages about external and internal realities as do measured results, our views about the relationships that exist between the knowable and the unfathomable change. But, above all, the portrait that we sketch of ourselves for ourselves, of humans as ourselves, changes: the belief that we are created "after" the ultimate "likeness" of God will be expunged from us completely. Yet, at the same time, we can still recognize and acknowledge how great and how wonderful the world is, of which we are a part and in which we take part. Just this, as Karl von Frisch writes, "leads to reverence before the unknown, and whoever gives such feelings a form on which he finds a firm footing for leading his life, he is on the right path." Together with the recognition that we are fully and completely of this world and not just in this world comes the recognition that we are charged with the full responsibility for it. I see human beings differently from the way Jacques Monod sees them — as lonely strangers at the edge of the universe — and I see them differently from the way transcendental idealism pictures them — as directly opposed to a fundamentally unknowable world. We humans are only an ephemeral link in the chain of the live and the living; there are good reasons for the assumption that we are but a developmental phase on the way to becoming truly humane beings. We are still allowed a little time to hope that this may be so.

Afterword: The Credo of a Natural Scientist

I feel pressed to write an epilogue addressed to all those who regard an exponent of evolutionary epistemology as being a crass materialist because he does not utter the word "God." In the Ten Commandments is written "Thou shalt not take the name of the Lord thy God in vain." I experience a deep inhibition to naming Him at all; most especially, I find the repeated use of the masculine personal pronouns very near to being a blasphemous presumption, even if these are written with capital letters. I feel it to be just as presumptuous when someone speaks — no matter how naive the person may be or how reverentially this is done — about an "encounter with God." Socrates, according to Plato, sensed something similar to this inhibition since he limited himself to speaking about "something godlike."

It appears to be impossible to convince esoteric ideationalists that our endeavors to know this world in all its secular worldliness, to the extent that it is possible for us to know it, do not signify a renunciation of everything transcendent. Still more difficult, as Nicolai Hartmann has emphasized, is to make comprehensible that the transcendent is simply gainsaid if one fetches the world of platonic ideas down from its heights beyond space and time and one then maintains that those ideas, as inborn images of the ideal and as innate goal-oriented driving forces, intervene in the course of what happens in the world. In the first part of this book I made every imaginable effort to show that no well-thought-through concept forms the basis of the creative happenings that occur in this world. The development has been in process over billions of years, and the living world has evolved, consequentially, step by step.

Writing inspired and really wonderful prose, Carl M. Feuerbach attempts to explode Darwin's "ape theory" in *Die Abstammung des Menschen im Lichte der Esoterik* [The descent of man in the light of the esoteric]: "Everything is planless and aimlessly 'improvised,' nothing is preprogrammed, the 'remarkable primate man' no god-willed exception! Extemporaneously, shooting from the hip so to say, in an unrefereed free-for-all of fantasizing forces, nature gropes her way along within an impervious fog, through 'natural selection in the struggle for survival,' through random vagrant chances and mutations among the ever-present external circumstances of a hostile environment toward an unwilled and uncertain distant future."

Here, in an attempt to exaggerate Darwin's theory on the origin of species to the point of absurdity, is expressed with remarkable poetic power what creative evolution actually does. Whatever the creative force may be that leads the never-before-extant higher organic form toward coming into being out of the lower organic form, this force creates "extemporaneously"! How else should the immanent creator bring forth his creation? He is not the actor who declaims the words and phrases some great author has written down; he himself is the poet who speaks here. He is not the performing musician who interprets the work of a composer; he himself is the composer who fantasizes an unconducted improvisation. I see the creative accomplishments of which highly gifted humans are capable as special cases of the universal creative process, that game played by everyone against everyone else, from which wells up all that has never been before. If the expression that humans are the likenesses of God contains any kind of truth, it is in respect to these creative acts.

Whoever believes in a god — and be it a belief in that jealous God of Abraham appointed with the characteristics of a choleric tribal chief — knows, in any case, more about the essence of the cosmos than does every ontological reductionist. Even the most naive monotheist who envisages a loving God as a benign father figure is fortified against a blindness for values. Even if he believes that his all-powerful and all-knowing God will, in the last instance, let all things work out to the good and to His own glory, he cannot overlook the satanically erroneous developments going on now. At the worst he will doubt the all-powerfulness of God because he has the existence of evil paraded everywhere before his very eyes. The content of truth in monotheism will hold the believer, in his practical actions, steady on the right path; the categorical commandments he has received from his God prove to be identical with those we also strive to obey.

What does offend me deeply about esoteric thinking is the truly sacrilegious presumptuousness of its projected image of the human. The idea that the human being is what was, from the very beginning, intended — the firmly fixed objective of all evolutionary development — seems to me to be *the* paradigm of that bedazzled pride which goes before a fall. If I had to believe that an all-powerful God had created humans as they are represented by an average of our species today *intentionally*, as they are, I would in truth be in despair about God. If these beings who are often not only so evil in their collective actions but also so dumb are supposed to be the likenesses of God, I then must say: "What a pitiful God!" Fortunately, however, I know from reckoning in geologic measurements of time that we humans have only just recently been anthropoid apes; I know, in addition, about the dangers for the human soul that have been precipitated by the rapid development of the human mind; and I know something more: that many of these dangers are caused, quite unambiguously, by sicknesses that are, at least in principle, curable. Axiomatically it is not possible to foretell if *Homo sapiens* will perish or survive; we are obligated to struggle for survival, for existence, for life.

Unforetellability is, however, an inalienable aspect of everything living. A closed system in which all of the processes are, in principle, predictable, as, for example, Nietzsche outlines in his philosophy of the eternal recurrence, is the most horrible of all horrors, because a closed system is, by definition, a nonliving system. But such a closed system does not exist, and it is not biology that has delivered us from this horror, but modern physics. It exceeds the capacities of human thinking to comprehend in what relationship human freedom stands to the unforetellability of what happens in the world. Certainly, however, it is possible to understand that in a predestined world, that is, in a world of events that are predetermined, there would be no place for human freedom.

Bibliography

Abel, O. *Lehrbuch der Paläozoologie.* Jena: G. Fischer, 1920.

Baerends, G. P., and R. H. Drent. "The Herring Gull's Egg." *Behavior* 17 (Supplement): 1970.

Bally G. *Vom Ursprung und von den Grenzen der Freiheit, eine Deutung des Spieles bei Tier und Mensch.* Basel: Birkhäuser, 1945.

Beebe, W. *The Arcturus Adventure.* New York/London: Putnam, 1926.

Berger, P. L., and T. Luckmann. *The Social Construction of Reality.* New York: Doubleday, 1966. (*Die gesellschaftliche Konstruktion der Wirklichkeit.* Frankfurt: Fischer, 1980.)

Boltzmann, L. *Populäre Schriften* (E. Broda, editor). Braunschweig: Vieweg, 1979.

Bridgeman, P. W. "Remarks on Niels Bohr's Talk." *Daedalus,* Spring 1958.

Brunswik, E. "Scope and Aspects of the Cognitive Problem." In T. S. Brunner et al. (editors), *Contemporary Approaches to Cognition.* Cambridge: Harvard University Press, 1957.

Bubenik, A. B. "The Significance of Antlers in the Social Life of the Cervidae." *Deer* 1 (1968): 208–214.

Bühler, K. *Handbuch der Psychologie,* Part I: *Die Struktur der Wahrnehmung.* Jena 1922.

Campbell, D. T. "Evolutionary Epistemology." In P. A. Schilpp (editor),

244 · *Bibliography*

The Philosophy of Karl Popper. La Salle, Ill.: Open Court Publications, 1966.

―――. "Pattern Matching as an Essential in Distal Knowing." In K. R. Hammond (editor), *The Psychology of Egon Brunswik.* New York: Holt, Rinehart and Winston, 1966.

Carson, R. *Silent Spring.* Boston: Houghton Mifflin, 1962. (*Der stumme Frühling.* Munich: Biederstein, 1962.)

Chargaff, E. *Unbegreifliches Geheimnis.* Stuttgart: Klett-Cotta, 1980.

Chomsky, N. *Language and Mind.* New York: Harcourt Brace Jovanovich, 1972. (*Sprache und Geist.* Frankfurt: Suhrkamp, 1970.)

Czerwenka-Wenkstetten, G. "Das 'leere' Gesicht." Lecture, 1977.

Darwin, C. *On the Origin of Species . . .* London: John Murray, 1859.

―――. *The Expression of Emotions in Man and Animals.* London: John Murray, 1872. (*Der Ausdruck der Gefühle bei Tier und Mensch.* Düsseldorf: Rau, 1964.)

Dawkins, R. *The Selfish Gene.* Oxford University Press, 1976. (*Das egoistische Gen.* Berlin/Heidelberg/New York: Springer, 1978.)

Eigen, M., and R. Winkler. *Das Spiel. Naturgesetze steuern den Zufall.* Munich/Zurich: Piper, 1975. (*Laws of the Game. How the Principles of Nature Govern Chance.* New York: Knopf, 1981.)

Erikson, E. H. "Ontogeny of Ritualization in Man." *Philosophical Transactions of the Royal Society* (London) 251 (1966): 337–349.

Festetics, A. *Kulturethologische und ökologische Aspekte pannonischer Volkstrachten.* In preparation.

Feuerbach, C. M. *Die Abstammung des Menschen im Lichte der Esoterik.* Privately printed, 1976.

Frankl, V. E. *Der Mensch vor der Frage nach dem Sinn.* Munich/Zurich: Piper, 1979.

Freud, S. *Gesammelte Werke.* 18 vols. London: Imago, 1950. (*Standard Edition of the Complete Psychological Works of Sigmund Freud,* J. Strachey, editor. London: Hogarth Press.)

Freyer, H. *Schwelle der Zeiten.* Stuttgart: Deutsche Verlagsanstalt, 1965.

―――. *Theorie des gegenwärtigen Zeitalters.* Stuttgart: Deutsche Verlagsanstalt, 1967.

Frisch, K. von. *Tanzsprache und Orientierung der Bienen.* Berlin/Heidelberg/New York: Springer, 1965.

―――. "Honeybees: Do They Use Direction and Distance Information Provided by Their Dancers?" *Science* 158 (1968): 1072–76.

Fromm, E. *Anatomie der menschlichen Destruktivität.* Stuttgart: Deutsche Verlagsanstalt, 1974.

Gehlen, A. *Der Mensch, seine Natur und seine Stellung in der Welt.* Berlin: Junker und Dürrhaupt, 1940.

Hahn, K. "Die List des Gewissens." In *Erziehung und Politik, Minna Specht zu ihrem 80. Geburtstag.* Frankfurt: Öffentliches Leben, 1960.

Hargreaves, R. Verbal communication.

Harlow, H. F. "Primary Affectional Patterns in Primates." *American Journal of Orthopsychiatry* 30 (1960).

Harlow, H. F., and M. K. Harlow. "The Effect of Rearing Conditions on Behavior." *Menninger Clinic Bulletin* 26 (1962): 213–244.

———. "Social Deprivation in Monkeys." *Scientific American* 207 (1962): 137–146.

Harlow, H. F., M. K. Harlow, and D. R. Meyer. "Learning Motivated by a Manipulation Drive." *Journal of Experimental Psychology* 40 (1950): 228–234.

Hartmann, M. *Allgemeine Biologie.* Jena: G. Fischer, 1933.

———. *Die philosophischen Grundlagen der Naturwissenschaften.* Jena: G. Fischer, 1948.

Hartmann, N. *Der Aufbau der realen Welt.* Berlin: de Gruyter, 1964.

———. *Teleologisches Denken.* Berlin: de Gruyter, 1966.

Hassenstein, B. *Biologische Kybernetik.* Heidelberg: Quelle & Meyer, 1965.

———. "Kybernetik und biologische Forschung." In *Handbuch der Biologie,* I, 631–719. Frankfurt: Athenaion, 1966.

———. *Verhaltensbiologie des Kindes.* Munich/Zurich: Piper, 1973.

Hediger, H. "Zur Biologie und Psychologie der Flucht bei Tieren." *Biologisches Zentralblatt* 54 (1934): 21–40.

———. *Wildtiere in Gefangenschaft.* Basel: Schwabe, 1942. (*Wild Animals in Captivity: An Outline of the Biology of Zoological Gardens.* New York: Dover, 1965.)

———. *Skizzen zu einer Tierpsychologie im Zoo und im Zirkus.* Zurich: Gutenberg, 1954. (*Studies of the Psychology and Behavior of Captive Animals in Zoos and Circuses.* London: Butterworth, 1955.)

Heinroth, O. "Beiträge zur Biologie, insbesondere Psychologie und Ethologie der Anatiden." In *Verhandlungen des 5. Internationalen Ornithologischen Kongresses,* Berlin, 1910.

———. "Über bestimmte Bewegungsweisen der Wirbeltiere." In *Sitzungsbericht der Gesellschaft der naturforschenden Freunde,* Berlin, 1930.

Heinroth, O., and M. Heinroth. *Die Vögel Mitteleuropas.* Berlin-Lichterfelde: Behrmüller, 1924–1928.

Heisenberg, W. *Der Teil und das Ganze. Gespräche im Umkreis der Atomphysik.* Munich/Zurich: Piper, 1969.

Holst, E. von. *Zur Verhaltensphysiologie bei Tieren und Menschen. Gesammelte Abhandlungen I und II.* Munich/Zurich: Piper, 1969–1970. (*The Behavioural Physiology of Animals and Man. The Selected Papers of Erich von Holst.* London: Methuen, 1973–1974.)

Huxley, A. *Brave New World.* New York: Harper & Row, 1932.

———. *Brave New World Revisited.* London: Chatto & Windus, 1959. (*Schöne Neue Welt — Dreißig Jahre Danach.* Munich/Zurich: Piper, 1976.)

Huxley, J. S. *Evolution, the Modern Synthesis.* New York: Harper & Row, 1942.

———. "A Discussion on Ritualization of Behaviour in Animals and Man." *Philosophical Transactions of the Royal Society* (London) 251, Series B, No. 772.

Kant, I. *Kritik der reinen Vernunft.* Neuausgabe der 2. Auflage von 1787, Band III, Kants Werke. Berlin: de Gruyter, 1968. (*Critique of Pure Reason.* B172–B173. New York: St. Martin's Press, 1963.)

Klages, L. *Der Geist als Widersacher der Seele.* Bonn: Bouvier, 1981.

Kneutgen, J. "Beobachtung Über die Anpassung von Verhaltensweisen an gleichförmige akustische Reize." *Zur Tierpsychologie* 21 (1964): 763–779.

———. "Eine Musikform und ihre biologische Funktion. Über die Wirkungsweise der Wiegenlieder." *Zeitschrift für experimentale und angewandte Psychologie* 17:2 (1970): 245–265.

Koehler, O. " 'Zählende' Vögel und vorsprachliches Denken." *Zoologische Anzeiger* Supplement 13 (1949): 129–238.

———. "Vom unbenannten Denken." *Zoologische Anzeiger* Supplement 16 (1952): 202–211.

———. "Vorbedingungen und Vorstufen userer Sprache bei Tieren." *Zoologische Anzeiger* Supplement 18 (1954): 327–341.

Koenig, O. *Kultur und Verhaltensforschung: Einführung in die Kulturethologie.* Munich: Deutscher Taschenbuchverlag, 1970.

Köhler, W. *Intelligenzprüfungen an Menschenaffen.* Berlin: Springer, 1921. (*The Mentality of Apes.* Rev. 2d ed. London: Routledge & Kegan Paul, 1973.)

Konishi, M. "Effects of Deafening on Song Development in Two Species of Juncos." *Condor* 66 (1964): 85–102.

———. "Effects of Deafening on Song Development of American Robins and Black-Headed Grosbeaks." *Zur Tierpsychologie* 22 (1965): 584–599.

———. "The Role of Auditory Feedback in the Control of Vocalization in the White-Crowned Sparrow." *Zur Tierpsychologie* 22 (1965): 770–783.

Kramer, G. "Macht die Natur Konstruktionsfehler?" *Wilhelmshavener Vorträge, Schriftenreihe der Norwestdeutsche Universitätsgesellschaft* 1 (1949): 1–19.

Kühn, A. *Die Orientierung der Tiere im Raum.* Jena: G. Fischer, 1919.

Kuhn, T. S. *Die Struktur wissenschaftlicher Revolutionen.* Frankfort: Suhrkamp, 1967.

Küppers, B.-O. *Evolutionstheoretische und ethische Aspekte der ökologischen Krise.* Göttingen: Max-Planck-Institut fur Biophysikalische Chemie, 1982.

Lagerlöf, S. *Wunderbare Reise des kleinen Nils Holgersson mit den Wildgänsen.* Munich: Nymphenburger, 1906–1907. (*The Wonderful Adventures of Nils.* New York: Doubleday, Page, 1907.)

Lawick-Goodall, H. van, and J. van Lawick-Goodall. *Innocent Killers.* Boston: Houghton Mifflin, 1971. (*Unschuldige Mörder.* Reinbeck: Rowohlt, 1972.)

Lawick-Goodall, J. van. "The Behavior of Free-living Chimpanzees in the Gombe Stream Reserve." *Animal Behavior Monographs* 1:3 (1968): 161–311.

———. *In the Shadow of Man.* London: Collins, 1971.

———. *Wilde Schimpansen.* Reinbeck: Rowohlt, 1971.

Lorenz, K. "Kants Lehre vom Apriorischen im Lichte gegenwärtiger Biologie." *Blätter für Deutsche Philosophie* 15 (1941).

———. *Das sogenannte Böse.* Vienna: Borotha-Schoeler, 1963.

———. *Über tierisches und menschliches Verhalten, Gesammelte Abhandlungen I und II.* Munich/Zurich: Piper, 1965. (*Studies in Animal and Human Behaviour.* 2 vols., London: Methuen, 1971.)

———. *On Aggression.* New York: Harcourt, Brace & World, 1966.

———. "The Enmity Between Generations and Its Probable Causes." *Studium Generale* 23 (1970): 963–997.

———. *Die acht Todsünden der zivilisierten Menschheit.* Munich: Piper, 1973. (*Civilized Man's Eight Deadly Sins.* New York: Harcourt Brace Jovanovich, 1974.)

———. *Die Rückseite des Spiegels.* Munich/Zurich: Piper, 1973. (*Behind the Mirror.* London: Methuen, 1977.)

———. *Analogy as a Source of Knowledge.* 1973 Nobel Prize Lecture. Stockholm: The Nobel Foundation, 1974.

———. *Die Vorstellung einer zweckgerichteten Weltordnung.* Vienna: Austrian Academy of Science, 1976.

———. *Vergleichende Verhaltensforschung: Grundlagen der Ethologie.* Vienna/New York: Springer, 1978. (*The Foundations of Ethology.* Vienna/New York: Springer, 1981.)

McDougall, W. *An Outline of Psychology.* London: Methuen, 1923.

MacKay, D. M. *Freedom of Action in a Mechanistic Universe.* Cambridge University Press, 1967.

Mayr, E. "Behavior and Systematics." In A. Roe and G. Simpson (editors), *Behavior and Evolution.* New Haven: Yale University Press, 1958.

———. *Artbegriff und Evolution*. Berlin: Parey, 1967.

———. "Evolution und Verhalten." *Verhandlungen der deutsche Zoologische Gesellschaft* 64 (Stuttgart) (1970): 322–366.

Metzger, W. *Psychologie*. Darmstadt: Steinkopff, 1953.

Monod, J. *Zufall und Notwendigkeit: Philosophische Fragen der modernen Biologie*. Munich/Zurich: Piper, 1971. (*Chance and Necessity: An Essay on the Natural Philosophy of Modern Biology*. New York: Knopf, 1971.)

Orwell, G. *Animal Farm*. Aylesbury: Hunt Barnard Printing, 1945. (*Farm der Tiere*. Frankfurt: Fischer, 1971.)

———. *Nineteen Eighty-Four*. New York: Harcourt Brace Jovanovich, 1949. (*Neunzehnundvierundachtzig. Ein utopischer Roman*. Zurich: Diana, 1949.)

Packard, V. *The Hidden Persuaders*. New York: McKay, 1957. (*Die geheimen Verführer*. Düsseldorf: Econ, 1958.)

Pietschmann, H. *Das Ende des naturwissenschaftlichen Zeitalters*. Vienna: Zsolnay, 1980.

Pittendrigh, C. "Perspectives in the Study of Biological Clocks." In *Perspectives in Marine Biology*. La Jolla: Scripps Institute for Oceanography, 1958.

Planck, M. "Sinn und Grenzen der exakten Naturwissenschaft." *Die Naturwissenschaft* 30 (1942).

Popper, K. R. *The Open Society and Its Enemies*. Princeton: Princeton University Press, 1950. (*Die offene Gesellschaft und ihre Feinde*. Bern/Munich: Francke, 1957.)

———. *The Poverty of Historicism*. London: Routledge & Kegan Paul, 1957.

———. *The Logic of Scientific Discovery*. New York: Harper & Row, 1962. (*Logik der Forschung*. Tübingen: Mohr, 1966.)

———. *Objective Knowledge*. Oxford: Clarendon Press, 1972.

———. "Scientific Reduction and the Essential Incompleteness of All Science." In *Studies in the Philosophy of Biology*. London: Macmillan, 1974.

Portielje, A. F. J. *Dieren zien en leeren kennen*. Amsterdam: Nederlandsche Keurboekerij, 1938.

Portmann, A. *Das Tier als soziales Wesen*. Zurich: Rhein-Verlag, 1953.

Riedl, R. *Die Strategie der Genesis: Naturgeschichte der realen Welt*. Munich/Zurich: Piper, 1976.

———. "Die Paarbildung bei einigen Zichliden II." *Zur Tierpsychologie* 5 (1941): 74–101.

Schmidt, W. "Qualitative und quantitative Untersuchungen am Verhalten von Haus- und Graugänsen." Dissertation, University of Düsseldorf, 1975.

Schulze, H. "Das Grenzsituationserlebnis in der Neurosentherapie." *Praxis der Psychotherapie* (1963).

———. *Nesthocker Mensch*. Stuttgart: Enke, 1977.

Seitz, A. "Die Paarbildung bei einigen Zichliden I." *Zur Tierpsychologie* 4 (1940): 40–84.

Skinner, B. F. *The Behavior of Organisms*. New York: Appleton-Century-Crofts, 1938.

———. "Reinforcement Today." *American Psychologist* 13 (1958): 94–99.

———. *Beyond Freedom and Dignity*. New York: Knopf, 1971. (*Jenseits von Freiheit und Würde*. Reinbek: Rowohlt, 1973.)

Snow, C. P. *The Two Cultures*. London: Cambridge University Press, 1959. (*Die zwei Kulturen: Literarische und naturwissenschaftliche Intelligenz*. Stuttgart: Klett, 1967.)

Spengler, O. *Der Untergang des Abendlandes*. Munich: Beck, 1918. (*The Decline of the West*. London: Allen & Unwin, 1926.)

Spitz, R. *Vom Saügling zum Kleinkind: Naturgeschichte der Mutter-Kind-Beziehungen im ersten Lebensjahr*. Stuttgart: Klett, 1965. (*The First Year of Life*. New York: International Universities Press, 1965.)

Sugiyama, Y. "Social Organization of Hanuman Langurs." In S. Z. Altmann, *Social Communications among Primates*. Chicago/London: University of Chicago Press, 1969.

Teilhard de Chardin, P. *Der Mensch im Kosmos*. Munich: Beck, 1959.

Tinbergen, N. *The Study of Instinct*. London: Oxford University Press, 1951. (*Instinktlehre: Vergleichende Verhaltensforschung angeborenen Verhaltens*. Berlin/Hamburg: Parey, 1952.)

———. *The Herring Gull's World*. London: Collins, 1953. (*Die Welt der Silbermöwe: Eine Untersuchung des Sozialverhaltens von Vögeln*. Göttingen: Musterschmidt, 1958.)

Toynbee, A. *A Study of History*. 3 vols. London: Oxford University Press, 1934. (*Der Gang der Weltgeschichte: Aufstieg und Verfall der Kulturen*. Stuttgart: Kohlhammer, 1950.)

Tretzel, E. "Imitation und Variation von Schäferpfiffen durch Haubenlerchen (*Galerida c. cristata L.*)." *Zur Tierpsychologie* 22 (1965): 784–809.

Uexküll, J. von. *Umwelt und Innenleben der Tiere*. Berlin, 1921.

Watson, J. B. *Psychology from the Standpoint of a Behaviorist*. Philadelphia: Lippincott, 1919. (*Der Behaviorismus*. Stuttgart: Deutsche Verlagsanstalt, 1930.)

Weiss, P. A. "The Living System: Determinism Stratified." In A. Koestler and J. R. Smythies (editors), *Beyond Reductionism*. London: Hutchinson, 1969. (*Das neue Menschenbild: Die Revolutionierung der Wissenschaft vom Leben*. Vienna/Munich: Molden, 1970.)

Weiss, P. A. (editor). *Hierarchically Organized Systems in Theory and Practice.* New York: Hafner, 1971.

Weisskopf, V. F. "Naturwissenschaft und Gesellschaft." *Physikalische Blätter* 27 (1970).

Wittgenstein, L. *Tractatus Logico-Philosophicus.* New York: Harcourt, Brace, 1922.

———. *Philosophical Investigations.* Oxford: Blackwell, 1953.

———. *Notebooks* 1914–1916. Oxford: Blackwell, 1961.

———. *Schriften.* 4 vols. Frankfurt: Suhrkamp, 1969.

Wuchterl, K., and A. Hübner. *Ludwig Wittgenstein in Selbstzeugnissen und Bilddokumenten.* Reinbek: Rowohlt, 1979.

Zahavi, A. "Reliability in Communication Systems and the Evolution of Altruism." In B. Stonehause and C. Perrins (editors), *Evolutionary Ecology.* London: Macmillan, 1977.

———. "The Lateral Display of Fishes: Bluff or Honesty in Signaling?" *Behavior Analysis Letters* 1 (1981): 233–235.

———. "Natural Selection, Sexual Selection and the Selection of Signals." In *Evolution Today: Proceedings of the Second International Congress of Systematic and Evolutionary Biology* (1981): 133–138.

Zuckmayer, C. *Der Rattenfänger: Eine Fabel.* Frankfurt am Main: Fischer, 1975.